HUGE
& HUGGABLE
MOCHIMOCHI

HUGE &
HUGGABLE
MOCHIMOCHI

20 Supersized Patterns for Big Knitted Friends

ANNA HRACHOVEC
PHOTOGRAPHY BY BRANDI SIMONS

POTTER
CRAFT

New York

Copyright © 2013 by Anna Hrachovec

All rights reserved.

Published in the United States by Potter Craft,
an imprint of Crown Publishing Group, a division of
Random House, Inc., New York

www.pottercraft.com
www.crownpublishing.com

POTTER CRAFT and colophon is a registered trademark of Random House, Inc.

Library of Congress Cataloging-in-Publication Data

Hrachovec, Anna.
  Huge & huggable mochimochi : 20 supersized patterns for big knitted friends /
Anna Hrachovec. — 1st ed.
    p. cm.
1. Amigurumi—Patterns. 2. Soft toy making. I. Title. II. Title: Huge and huggable
mochimochi.
  TT829.H726 2013
  745.592'4—dc23

ISBN: 978-0-385-34457-9
eISBN: 978-0-385-34458-6

Printed in China

Book design by Ken Crossland
Book photography by Brandi Simons and Anna Hrachovec
Cover photographs by Brandi Simons
Photographs on the following pages copyright © 2013 by Brandi Simons: 2, 4, 6,
8, 10, 18, 38, 43, 44, 49, 50, 56, 60, 64, 68, 72, 76, 82, 84, 86, 88, 94, 98, 101, 102,
106, 111, 112, 118, 124, 126, 130, 134, 138, 141, 146, 159
All other photographs copyright © 2013 by Anna Hrachovec

The author and publisher would like to thank the Craft Yarn Council of America for
providing the yarn weight standards and accompanying icons used in this book.
For more information, please visit www.YarnStandards.com.

10 9 8 7 6 5 4 3 2 1

First Edition

For my parents,
who inspire me to
think big

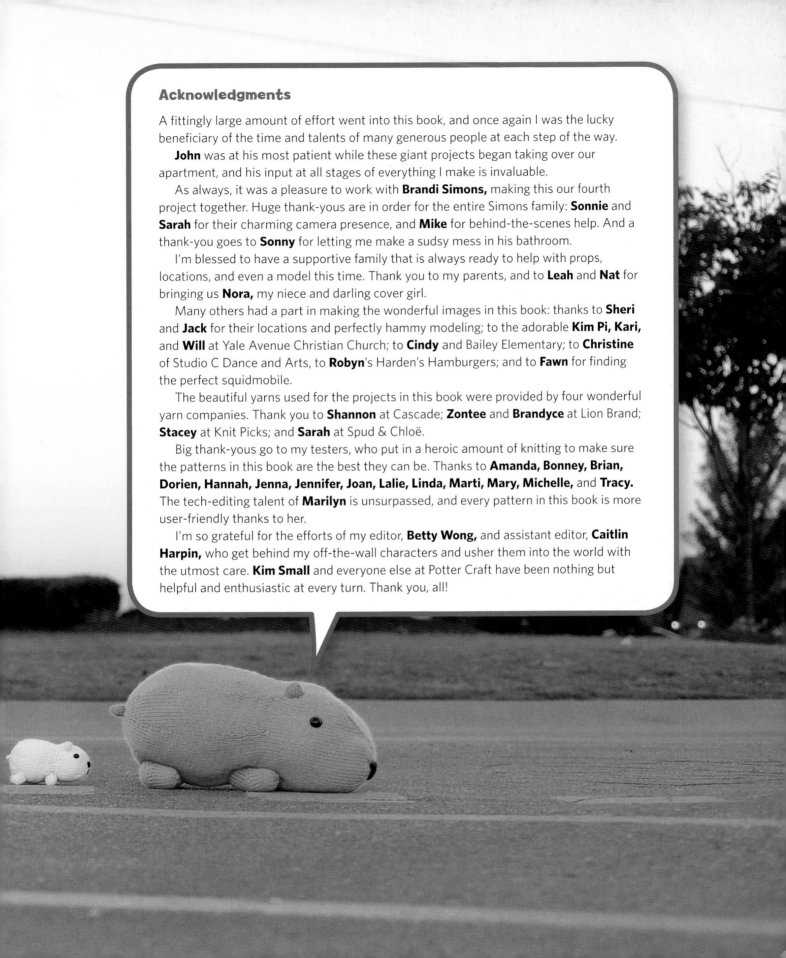

Acknowledgments

A fittingly large amount of effort went into this book, and once again I was the lucky beneficiary of the time and talents of many generous people at each step of the way.

John was at his most patient while these giant projects began taking over our apartment, and his input at all stages of everything I make is invaluable.

As always, it was a pleasure to work with **Brandi Simons,** making this our fourth project together. Huge thank-yous are in order for the entire Simons family: **Sonnie** and **Sarah** for their charming camera presence, and **Mike** for behind-the-scenes help. And a thank-you goes to **Sonny** for letting me make a sudsy mess in his bathroom.

I'm blessed to have a supportive family that is always ready to help with props, locations, and even a model this time. Thank you to my parents, and to **Leah** and **Nat** for bringing us **Nora,** my niece and darling cover girl.

Many others had a part in making the wonderful images in this book: thanks to **Sheri** and **Jack** for their locations and perfectly hammy modeling; to the adorable **Kim Pi, Kari,** and **Will** at Yale Avenue Christian Church; to **Cindy** and Bailey Elementary; to **Christine** of Studio C Dance and Arts, to **Robyn**'s Harden's Hamburgers; and to **Fawn** for finding the perfect squidmobile.

The beautiful yarns used for the projects in this book were provided by four wonderful yarn companies. Thank you to **Shannon** at Cascade; **Zontee** and **Brandyce** at Lion Brand; **Stacey** at Knit Picks; and **Sarah** at Spud & Chloë.

Big thank-yous go to my testers, who put in a heroic amount of knitting to make sure the patterns in this book are the best they can be. Thanks to **Amanda, Bonney, Brian, Dorien, Hannah, Jenna, Jennifer, Joan, Lalie, Linda, Marti, Mary, Michelle,** and **Tracy.** The tech-editing talent of **Marilyn** is unsurpassed, and every pattern in this book is more user-friendly thanks to her.

I'm so grateful for the efforts of my editor, **Betty Wong,** and assistant editor, **Caitlin Harpin,** who get behind my off-the-wall characters and usher them into the world with the utmost care. **Kim Small** and everyone else at Potter Craft have been nothing but helpful and enthusiastic at every turn. Thank you, all!

Contents

Introduction: Mega Mochis · 9

The Big Picture · 10

Get It Together: Materials & Tools · 12

Big Knits for Little Ones · 16

The Skinny on Gauge · 17

Large and in Charge: Basic Toy Knitting

Techniques · 20

More Power to You: Additional Techniques · 32

Colossal Critters · 36

Roary · 39

Nesting Birds · 45

Barry & Theo · 51

Squidpocalypse · 57

Capybara Caravan · 61

Magnified Minis · 66

Baby Cakes · 69

Oozy & Bristles · 73

Big Mike · 77

Arthur · 85

Roland · 89

Gentle Giants · 92

USS *Bubbles* · 95

Dawn · 99

Buddy Boy · 103

Cityzens · 107

Tree-o · 113

Practical Pals · 116

Lupe · 119

Squee · 127

King Shuffle · 131

Sleepbot 3000 · 135

Totes Adorbs · 139

Knitting Essentials · 142

How to Read Charts · 156

Resources · 158

Index · 160

Introduction:
Mega Mochis

There must be something in the Mochimochi Land water lately, because the toys keep getting bigger and bigger! It's a scientific fact: The size of the average mochi has nearly tripled, and this gigantic bunch shows no signs of slimming down.

That's good news for us knitters, because bigger toys mean there's more to love. The huge mochis in this book are the perfect size for hugging, bedtime snuggling, and joining you on the couch for movie night. These larger-than-life toys come with big personalities that match their massive size, of course. Whether it's a humongous hamburger, a colossal capybara, or a rotund sun, the cuteness contained in one supersized mochi is enough to brighten up an entire room.

Why knit a jumbo mochi? Well, what birthday party wouldn't be more fun with a big, squishy piñata that can hold a bucketload of candy? All the hipsters in Brooklyn want a hand-knitted monster truck, and so do their suburban little cousins. A giant pencil would be a perfect mascot for teachers, writers, and editors everywhere. And can you say "ultimate baby shower gift"? You'd be surprised at who among us "needs" a big knitted character in their life if you just ask around.

If you're already a toy knitter, the projects in this book will take your knitting to new levels of excitement, integrating fun techniques like colorwork, cables, bobbles, and more. Bigger toys mean more design elements, but these guys knit up more quickly than you'd expect with bulky yarns. And, as with all knitted toys, you can customize the size with your choice of yarn.

If you're new to toys or knitting in general, the tutorials in the front of the book and the knitting basics in the back are all you need to get started. Many of the projects include smaller versions, so you can start out with a little friend before tackling his big brother.

It's important to indulge in big, silly projects sometimes, and these are guaranteed to end with hugs!

The Big

Ready to knit your new main squeeze? Read on
to find out what you need and what to do with it
to start knittin' large.

Picture

GET IT TOGETHER: MATERIALS & TOOLS

Yarn

The yarn you use will determine if your toy is hairy or sleek, neutral or neon (and everything in between). If you find a cool yarn that's hand-dyed, variegated, or textured in an unusual way, don't be afraid to use it—toys are perfect projects for experimenting with unconventional fibers.

Your yarn, in combination with your needles, will also determine the size of your new friend. I use bulky to super bulky yarn for the jumbo-sized projects, but if you use a thinner yarn and smaller needles, your toys will be adorable smaller cousins to the full-size characters in this book.

Most of these projects require a hefty amount of yarn (anywhere from 3 to 13 skeins), but that doesn't mean you have to choose between knitting and putting food on the table. Some of my favorite bulky yarns are affordable acrylic varieties that come in exciting colors.

If you're wondering which type of yarn is right for you, read on to learn more about some of the more common fibers available.

Acrylic

Widely available in all craft stores, acrylic yarn is generally durable, affordable, and machine-washable. (I still recommend washing all toys by hand.) It can also be scratchy and tough to work with, but that has changed significantly in recent years as soft and beautiful acrylics have emerged. Acrylic is a great choice for knitting toys, so I encourage knitters to consider it as a low-cost option.

Wool

I love working with wool because of its soft, springy feel. There are lots of different varieties and blends of wool yarn available, and these can significantly affect the texture and price. Superwash wool, for example, has been treated for easier washing. Yarns that contain a blend of wool and synthetic fiber are generally affordable and easier to wash as well.

Cotton

Another natural fiber, cotton is a durable and washable option that is often a good choice for knitting for kids or people who are allergic to wool. I find it to be a tougher yarn to work with, but blends are also available that offer a variety of textures.

I've just scratched the surface of the huge variety of yarn that is available to knitters today. When people ask me what kind of yarn they should use to knit a toy, I tell them that I've never met a yarn that wouldn't make a great toy. It all depends on what kind of friend you want to create, whether it's a rough-and-tumble plaything, an heirloom for display, or a weird and woolly creature who will live in your bedroom.

Needles

Knitting needles are the tools that will transform your yarn into a cuddly character. Everyone is familiar with the classic pair of straight needles, but toy knitting magic happens with needles that allow you to knit in the round.

Double-Pointed Needles

With pointed tips at either end, double-pointed needles (DPNs, for short) are good for circular knitting in varying circumferences, and they're particularly helpful for knitting pieces with small circumferences. DPNs come in sets of five, although you will usually work with only four needles at a time—three needles to hold your stitches in a triangular configuration, and a fourth needle to knit with. You can also use two DPNs in place of straight needles to knit a small, flat piece.

Circular Needle

A versatile favorite, the circular needle is basically two needles connected seamlessly by a length of flexible cable.

You can use a circular needle for knitting a large number of stitches in a round, and smaller circumferences are also possible with a technique called magic loop knitting (page 22). Like DPNs, a circular needle can also double as a pair of straight needles when you need to knit a larger, flat piece.

Needle Materials

Needles come in a variety of materials, including wood, bamboo, metal, and plastic. Many local craft stores will let you try out different needles before buying, so that you can find the type that you're most comfortable with. My personal preference is for lightweight bamboo or wood DPNs and circular needles.

Needle Size

When determining your needle size, keep in mind that your stitches should be tighter when knitting toys than they need to be when knitting a garment. This is so that the stuffing doesn't show through the finished toy. There are standard recommended needle sizes for the different weights of yarn (Yarn Weight System, page 157), and most yarn also comes with a recommended needle size on a label—as a general rule, you should go down two or three sizes from these recommended needle sizes to knit toys.

Another way to pinpoint the right needle size for a project is to check your gauge against the gauge noted in a pattern (The Skinny on Gauge, page 17).

Needle Length

The length of needles you choose to use depends on the circumference size of your knitting. However, toy knitting involves a wide range of circumferences and stitch counts within a single pattern, so it's important to be equipped in a way that allows for flexibility with circumference size. A length of 7" (18cm) for DPNs and between 30" and 46" (76–117cm) for a circular needle, along with knowledge of two magic loop knitting techniques (page 22), will be suitable for knitting all the patterns in this book.

Needle Options: Circular Needle, DPNs, or Both?

If you aren't already well-stocked with various needles, you may be wondering which types of needles (and which lengths) are essential for the projects in this book. The types of needles depend on whether you are comfortable using both DPNs and a circular needle.

If you prefer to use a circular needle only, you can skip the DPNs altogether. Instead, use a circular needle of 30–46" (76–117cm) in length and the magic loop knitting techniques (page 22) for sections of small-circumference knitting. DPNs are still best for knitting I-cords (which are used in many patterns in this book), but not necessary if your needle options are limited.

If you are comfortable using both DPNs and a circular needle, I recommend a set of five DPNs 7–8" (18–20.5cm) long, in combination with a circular needle. You will usually only use four DPNs at a time, but if you prefer to knit with DPNs for a longer time before switching to the circular needle, use five needles to work a bigger circumference before making the switch. The circular needle in this case may be shorter than what you would need for magic loop knitting, although the ideal length depends on the size of the project.

Some of the smaller projects in this book can be knit using DPNs only.

Eyes

Eyes are the small but crucial detail that will transform your toy from a squishy blob into a new friend. As with yarn choice, the type of eyes, along with their size and placement, can give your toys wildly different personalities. Eyes can be made of yarn, beads, buttons, felt, or a variety of other materials.

I use extra-big plastic "safety eyes" in most of the projects in this book. They're easy to use by snapping in place with a backing, and they are usually good at staying put. Despite the name, however, they're not safe for children aged three and under. A simple baby-safe alternative is to embroider eyes using a contrasting-colored yarn. (See Big Knits for Little Ones, on page 17.)

For projects that use a pillow in place of stuffing, I recommend using buttons, since they will lie flat against the pillow.

Stuffing

Like yarn and needles, stuffing comes in a variety of materials: wool, bamboo, and my preferred material, polyester. Each one has a different weight and texture; for example, wool is denser and gives a toy a nice, heavy weight, while polyester is springy and light. With large toys, the amount of yarn involved already contributes a lot of weight, so using a lightweight stuffing will keep your toy from getting very heavy.

Your choice of stuffing also depends on what kind of wear the toy will get. If you expect that the toy will need to be washed often, then polyester is a good choice because it dries quickly and is less likely to become moldy.

Tools

You won't use all these tools for every pattern, but it's still a good idea to have them on hand.

Scissors

Scissors are a must, and a pair with a pointed tip is best to use with knitting projects.

Tapestry Needle

Like a jumbo-sized sewing needle, a tapestry needle is used with yarn for seaming, embroidery details, and weaving in loose ends. Some varieties have a bent tip, which makes it easier to go in and out of a knitted piece.

Stitch Markers

Stitch markers help you remember where the rounds in your knitting begin and end, and they are also sometimes used midway through a round to help keep track of repeating stitch patterns. You can buy small plastic rings, or make your own by simply tying a small piece of contrasting-colored yarn in a loop.

Tape Measure or Ruler

This is essential for checking gauge or for measuring pieces that need to fit together.

Stitch Holder

A stitch holder allows you to hold live stitches temporarily so that you can come back to them later. If you don't have a large safety pin–shaped holder, you can use a spare needle or simply thread a piece of waste yarn through the live stitches and tie the ends together.

Crochet Hook

A crochet hook is useful for attaching hair to a toy, fringe to a scarf, and for picking up stitches dropped accidentally. Use one that's approximately the same size as the knitting needles you're using.

Cable Needle

A cable needle is a different sort of stitch holder that allows you to work cables by twisting one group of stitches around another. You can use an extra DPN in place of a cable needle.

Stitch Counter

A stitch counter helps you keep track of the row or round you're on; the typical one is an easy-to-use clicking device. A low-tech alternative is making hash marks on a piece of paper. A high-tech alternative is to download one of the stitch counter apps now available for mobile devices.

Straight Pins

Straight pins are helpful when you're attaching pieces together, so that you can get the spacing right before you start stitching, and (for bigger pieces) hold the pieces in place as you attach them.

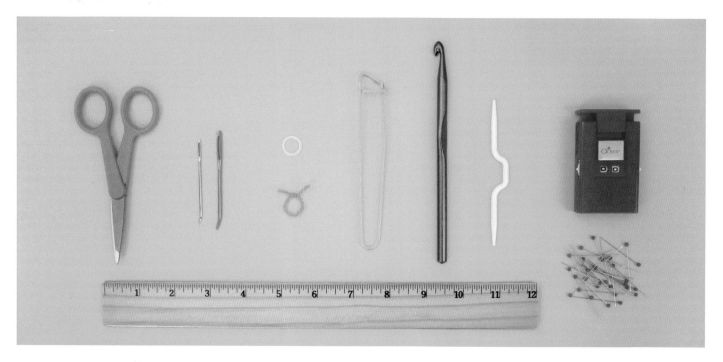

BIG KNITS FOR LITTLE ONES

If your monstrous mochi will be pals with a child aged three or younger, make sure the toy is age-appropriate by following these guidelines.

- Embroider eyes with a contrasting-colored yarn. Plastic eyes, although commonly called "safety eyes," can still get loose and are not safe for babies and toddlers.
- Make seams extra secure by sewing around them twice, and weaving loose ends through the toy multiple times to prevent pieces from getting loose and becoming choking hazards.
- Many of the toys in this book are bigger than a small child; babies and toddlers should be supervised when playing with large toys.

Keep It Clean

A toy that gets lots of love will need occasional cleaning. Even if the yarn that you use is "washable," I recommend spot cleaning for all but the biggest messes. If your toy needs some deep cleaning, gently hand-wash it and make sure it air-dries thoroughly before storing it.

Like knitted garments, when not in use, knitted toys should be stored in a cool, dry place.

THE SKINNY ON GAUGE

Checking gauge is the best way to see if your finished project will be the same size as the sample that appears in the book. It's essential when you're knitting a sweater or other wearable item, but less essential when knitting a toy. My rule of thumb is to go down two to three needle sizes from the size recommended on the yarn's label.

I do recommend a quick gauge check for some projects that need to have particular dimensions, such as the toys in this book that are meant to fit over pillows.

Checking gauge is a simple process that takes only a few minutes and a little math:

1. Using the yarn you have chosen for a project and the needle size called for in the pattern, knit a flat square about 5" by 5" (12.5cm x 12.5cm) in stockinette stitch (knit on the right side, purl on the wrong side).
2. Lay the square flat without stretching it—it's helpful to pin it to an ironing board or another surface so it won't slip around—and use a ruler or tape measure to determine how many stitches and how many rows there are per inch or centimeter.
3. If your stitch/row counts are significantly smaller than in the given gauge (i.e., your knitting is looser than in the sample), switch to a smaller-sized needle and try again. If your stitch/row counts are significantly larger than in the given gauge (i.e., your knitting is tighter than in the sample), you can try using a larger-sized needle. Another way to adjust the gauge is to use a different yarn that is closer in weight to that suggested in the pattern.

Even huge mochis like to see the latest blockbusters at the movie theater. Their all-time favorites are *Big*, *Giant*, and *Sleepless in Seattle*.

LARGE AND IN CHARGE: BASIC TOY KNITTING TECHNIQUES

New to knitting big toys? Bulk up your knowledge of three-dimensional knitting in this section. You can find knitting basics and general techniques in Knitting Essentials (page 142).

Using Double-Pointed Needles

Even the largest toys have to start out small. Double-pointed needles (DPNs) help you start out with a small number of stitches before increasing the stitch number and switching to a circular needle. To use a circular needle in place of DPNs, see Magic Loop Knitting (page 22).

DPNs look more complicated than they are. The trick is to focus on the two needles that you're working with at any given time, and let the other needles hold your other stitches until you come around to them.

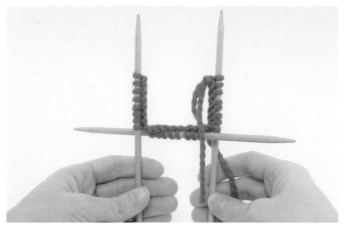

❶ Begin by using just one needle to cast on all your stitches. Then, distribute the new stitches onto three needles, slipping them purlwise onto the new needles. Hold the needle with the attached yarn in your right hand. To make sure that you aren't twisting the stitches, align the bumpy cast-on edge to the insides of the needles.

❷ If you are using a stitch marker to keep track of the beginning of your rounds, slip the marker onto the needle in your right hand, and knit the first stitch from the left needle onto the right. If you're beginning with a small number of stitches (see Beginning with a Small Number of Stitches, opposite), you can do this step at the beginning of a later round, after you have increased the total number of your stitches.

❸ Now use a fourth needle to knit the stitches on the needle in your left hand. Pull the yarn tightly between the needles to prevent the first stitch from being too loose.

❹ When you finish knitting from the needle in your left hand, the stitches will all end up on the right-hand needle. Slide these stitches down a bit on the right-hand needle so that they won't slip off. Rotate the needles slightly in a clockwise direction, and continue knitting the stitches from the next needle to the left onto your newly empty needle.

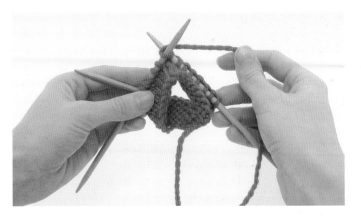

5 Continue knitting from the needle in your left hand to the needle in your right, around and around, slipping the stitch marker along when you come to it. (Every time you come to the marker, you have just finished one round of knitting.) After knitting a few rounds, you will see a three-dimensional shape take form.

6 Sometimes a column of loose stitches (often called a "ladder") may form because of the gaps between the needles. One way to avoid this and keep tension even is to slip the stitches around the needles every few rounds. Do this by setting aside the fourth needle and knitting 2 stitches directly from one needle to another before continuing. (Repeat with every needle in one round to shift all the stitches around.)

Beginning with a Small Number of Stitches

Many of the pieces you will knit in this book begin with 6 or fewer stitches on the needles, and then increase the number in the first round. The easiest way to start out with a small number of stitches is to begin by knitting the first round as you would an I-cord.

1 After casting on, leave your stitches on just one DPN, and slide them to the right end of the needle with the working yarn attached to the leftmost stitch.

2 Pull the attached yarn behind the needle and, pulling tightly, knit the first stitch onto a second needle. (In most patterns, you will work a kfb increase with this stitch.) Continue to work the rest of the stitches from the left needle onto the right.

3 Once you have finished knitting the stitches on the needle and have increased their total number, distribute the stitches onto three DPNs and continue knitting in the round with a fourth needle.

Using a Circular Needle

Whether you switch to a circular needle midway in a piece after using DPNs, or you are starting a new piece by casting onto a circular needle, the idea is the same as using DPNs: knitting in a continuous round in a counterclockwise direction.

Magic Loop Knitting

Magic loop is a technique that will give you the most flexibility in the circumference size (or number of stitches) that you're working with, making it ideal for knitting large toys, which involve a wide range of stitch counts to form solid three-dimensional shapes. Usually, DPNs can be replaced by a circular needle and this technique.

Instead of choosing a needle that's shorter than the circumference of your knitting (as is the conventional way to use a circular needle), start with a longer needle. I've found that a needle length between 30" and 46" (76–117cm) works well with almost any project.

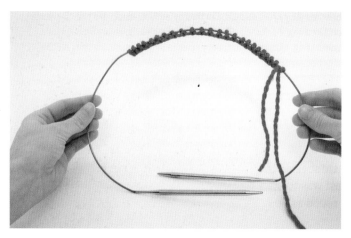

❶ After casting on the stitches, slide all the stitches down onto the flexible cable.

❷ Divide the stitches into two groups, and fold the cable in half between them, with the working yarn attached to the group on the bottom. Grab onto the cable between the two groups of stitches.

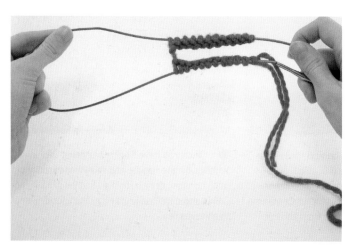

❸ Pull the cable out between the stitches until you have pulled out a big loop.

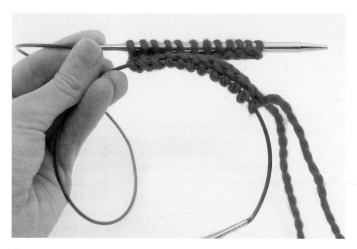

❹ Slide the top group of stitches (the group without the yarn attached) down to one end of the needle. Leave the bottom group of stitches on the cable, while keeping the loop pulled out between the two groups. Make sure that the bumpy cast-on edge is aligned on the insides of the stitches to prevent twisted stitches.

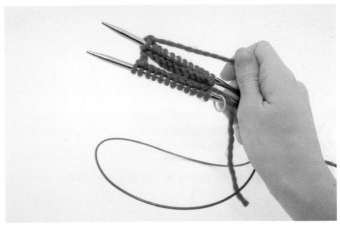

⑤ Pick up the empty end of the needle with your right hand, and place a stitch marker onto it. Then, knit the stitches from the left end of the needle onto the empty right end, pulling the yarn tightly to join the stitches into a round.

⑥ Once you finish knitting this group of stitches, slide the other group of stitches down to the other end of the needle, so that the two groups of stitches are on the two ends of the needle. Check that the cast-on edge is still aligned without any twists.

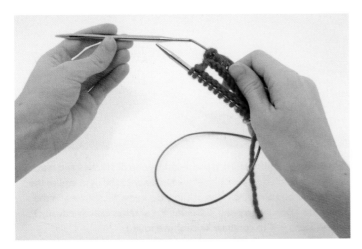

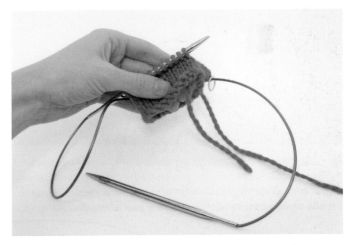

⑦ Slide the stitches you just finished knitting (with the yarn attached) down onto the cable.

⑧ Flip the needle around so that the stitches are positioned as they were in Step 5, and knit the second group of stitches to complete one round of knitting. Repeat Steps 5–8 to continue knitting in the round. After a few rounds, you will see a circular piece start to take shape.

Partial Magic Loop

If you have too many stitches on the needle for magic loop, but not enough to use your circular needle in the conventional way, you can use a combination of the two techniques that I call partial magic loop.

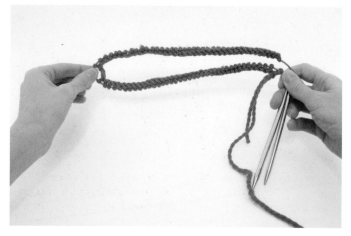

❶ After casting on the stitches, slide all the stitches to the center of the cable. Divide the stitches into two groups, and fold the cable in half between them, with the working yarn attached to the group on the bottom.

Grasp the bit of cable between the two groups of stitches, and pull out a loop.

❷ Slide the stitches to either end of the needle. Hold the end with the attached yarn in your right hand, place a marker onto that needle, and begin knitting the stitches from the left end onto the right, joining them in a round. Make sure that the bumpy cast-on edge is aligned toward the middle.

❸ When you finish knitting the first group of stitches and you reach the loop of cable, locate the stitch marker on the other side, and pull out a loop of cable where the stitch marker is, sliding the stitches to the left of the loop down onto the end of the needle in your left hand as you do so.

❹ When you finish knitting the second group of stitches and reach the loop and stitch marker, place the marker onto the right end of the needle, and pull out a new loop of cable between the stitches on the other side. (Don't worry about dividing the stitches exactly equally.) Repeat Steps 3–4 to continue knitting in a round.

Stuffing and Closing Up

There are several ways to finish a piece, but the most common way in toy patterns is to draw the yarn through the last stitches and cinch them closed together. Unless it is open-ended, stuff the piece before closing it up.

❶ You should begin stuffing a few rounds before the end of the piece, when the opening is still big enough to reach inside. When stuffing a large toy, you may need to use more stuffing than you would expect in order to completely fill out the shape, including all nooks and crannies. Don't worry if your toy looks lumpy—it may just need a little massaging to get the right shape.

❷ When you are finished knitting and are ready to close up the piece, cut the yarn, leaving a tail of 6" to 12" (15–30.5cm). Thread the tail onto a tapestry needle. Beginning with the first stitch in the round, insert the tapestry needle purlwise through each of the stitches in order, slipping the stitches off the needles as you go. (The technique is the same if you were using a circular needle instead of DPNs.)

❸ Pull the end of the cut yarn tight to draw the stitches closed.

Weaving in Loose Ends

After finishing off a piece or attaching one piece to another, you'll have a loose tail of yarn that needs to be dealt with. You can either weave the tails in as you go, or deal with them all at once as a last step when finishing your toy.

❶ Thread the loose end onto a tapestry needle, and insert the needle back into the toy in the same place from which the tail emerges. (Inserting the needle in this spot prevents the tail from pulling on the toy's surface and making it puckered.)

❷ Bring the needle all the way out another side of the toy. Repeat Steps 1 and 2 several more times to ensure that the tail is sufficiently caught in the stuffing on the inside of the piece and won't come loose.

❸ When the end is sufficiently woven in, cut the yarn short, gently pressing on the toy so the end disappears inside.

Attaching Eyes

Your toy will really come alive when you give it eyes to look back at you with. I have several go-to ways to add eyes to a toy.

Plastic Safety Eyes

Safety eyes come with a backing that snaps in place to hold the eyes securely. Despite their name, safety eyes can come undone or can be pulled out between stitches, and so they should not be used in toys for kids ages three and younger.

You will need to insert the back of the eyes on the wrong side of your knitting, so you'll attach these eyes before you close up your toy's body.

After you've stuffed the body, insert the front halves of the eyes where you would like them on the toy. Be sure that you're happy with the placement—once you've attached the backing, it's difficult—sometimes impossible—to separate it from the front.

Reach inside the toy to snap the backs in place, with the flatter side of the backing facing the eye shaft.

Button Eyes

Button eyes are added after a piece is fully stuffed and closed up. Buttons with very large holes can be stitched on using yarn and a tapestry needle, but most need to be attached with thread and a sewing needle.

❶   Tie the thread to the body exactly where you want to place the eye. Make a secure knot.

❷   Place the button on top of the knot, and stitch the button to the body through the holes. You may find it helpful to pinch the body so that you can more easily stitch in and out of the buttonholes.

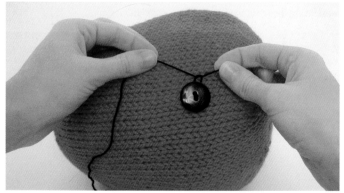

❸   When the button is securely attached with multiple stitches, insert the needle into a buttonhole and bring it out the underside of the button, on top of the body. Make a wide loop with the thread, and tie a knot around the underside of the button. A square knot will hold more securely.

Embroidered Eyes

Another simple way to add eyes is to embroider them on with yarn and a tapestry needle. This option is the best for toys that will be given to babies and toddlers.

Locate where you would like to place the eye, and decide how big you would like your eye to be.

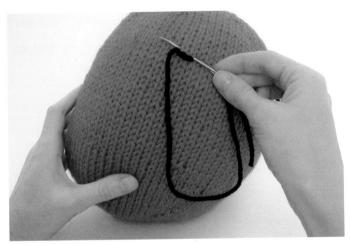

❶ Thread a piece of contrasting-colored yarn onto a tapestry needle. Insert the needle in the back of the body, and bring it out where you want the eye to begin. Because this yarn will stay in place with the stitches you make, you don't need to knot it.

❷ Insert the needle to the right of where the yarn emerges from the body, and bring it out again in the same place where you started. The width of this stitch will determine how big the eye will be.

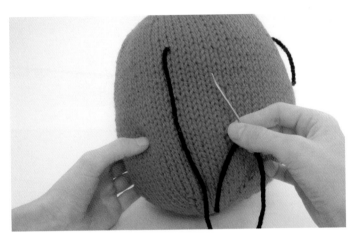

❸ Repeat Step 2 several more times, inserting the needle and bringing it out from the same place, so that the stitches overlap and the eye has some volume.

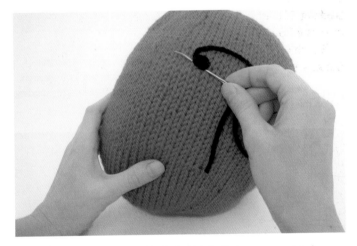

❹ To build the eye out vertically (which isn't always necessary), make more stitches just above and below the stitches that you just embroidered, until the eye looks circular.

Repeat the process to make a second eye, then weave in the loose ends of the yarn.

Perpendicular Mattress Stitch

Most of the seaming for the projects in this book will involve attaching three-dimensional pieces together, rather than flat pieces. On these occasions, use a combination of the previous techniques.

❶   To attach two three-dimensional pieces together, locate the place where you want them to be joined, and pin or hold them in place.

❷   Note that at the top and bottom, the stitches on the smaller piece line up horizontally with the stitches on the larger piece. Beginning at the top, use horizontal mattress stitch until the stitches no longer line up.

❸   For the next stitch of the larger piece, slip the needle diagonally down through the side of one knitted stitch and up through the middle of the stitch below it and to the left.

❹   Now switch to vertical-to-horizontal mattress stitch, slipping the needle under the bars on the larger body piece and the Vs on the smaller piece.

❺   When the stitches stop lining up vertical-to-horizontal, again make one or more diagonal stitches on the large piece, then switch back to horizontal mattress stitch for the bottom of the smaller piece. Continue to seam in a circle in this way until you come back to the place where you started. The result is a seamless join, with the smaller piece sticking straight out from the large one.

You can also use this technique to stitch a flat piece onto a three-dimensional piece. Just remember to start with some slack on the flat piece, since you will stitch on the outside of the piece and pull the outer edge underneath.

Back Stitch

Back stitch is another seaming technique that you can use to attach a flat piece to a three-dimensional piece. This simple stitching technique creates a secure seam.

❶ Overlap the two pieces that you want to attach together. Insert the tapestry needle straight down through both pieces, and bring it back up some distance away. Make the stitches the same length on top and underneath.

❷ Insert the needle back down into the same place where you inserted it in Step 1, so that the second stitch abuts the first. Again, bring the needle back up at a distance equal to the length of one stitch.

❸ Repeat Step 2 across the seam, maintaining an even tension throughout.

MORE POWER TO YOU: ADDITIONAL TECHNIQUES

Expand your toy-knitting know-how with these additional techniques that will come in handy for the projects in this book.

Reattaching Yarn to Live Stitches

When you need to attach a new piece of yarn, you can usually tie it to the end of the piece you have been working with and just keep knitting. In some cases, however, you need to reattach yarn to a live stitch without the help of another piece of yarn.

❶   Thread the end of the yarn onto a tapestry needle, and slip the needle through a stitch next to the first stitch that you will knit. Bring the needle out on the back, or purl, side of the piece, then weave the loose ends through a couple of stitches on the back of the piece.

❷   Loop the end of the yarn through itself to secure it.

Picking Up Stitches on a Three-Dimensional Piece

Another seamless way to add appendages or other features to a body is to pick up stitches on the body and knit outward.

❶   Decide where on the piece you want to pick up stitches. Depending on the placement of the stitches, you may need to turn the piece sideways or upside down. Beginning with the rightmost stitch, slip the tip of a double-pointed needle under the bar between knitted stitches, and place the yarn between the tip of the needle and the piece, with the loose end on the right.

❷   With the needle, pull the yarn from under the bar, creating a loop, as you would for a regular knit stitch.

❸   For subsequent stitches, repeat Steps 1 and 2 with the bar immediately to the left on the body.

Note: If you find it difficult to pick up stitches with a needle, use a crochet hook to pick up each stitch before slipping it onto the needle.

Picking Up Stitches around the Perimeter of a Piece

A handy shaping technique that adds structure to three-dimensional designs is to knit a flat piece, then pick up and knit the stitches around its sides. This allows you to create a boxy shape with circular knitting and minimal seaming.

The following photos show the stitches on double-pointed needles, but this same technique can be used with a circular needle instead.

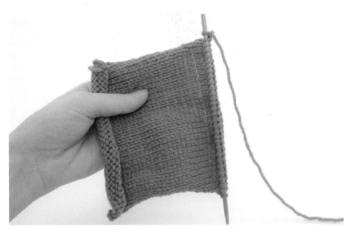

❶   After knitting a flat piece (usually a rectangle), work one more right-side row, ending up with the working yarn at the top left corner of the piece. Without turning the piece, rotate it 90 degrees clockwise, so that the adjacent side faces up, with the needle holding the live stitches to the right.

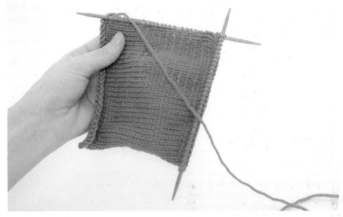

❷   Using the working yarn and a new needle, pick up and knit the specified number of stitches along this side edge from right to left, making sure to space the stitches as evenly as possible.

❸   When you come to the end of the side, rotate the piece again, and pick up and knit the specified number of stitches on the cast-on edge of the piece with another needle. (Note that the number of stitches to pick up may be different from the number of stitches that you cast on.)

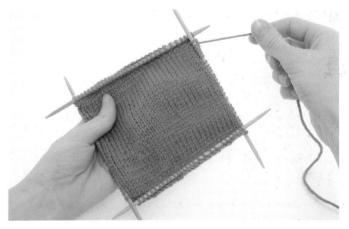

❹   Finish by rotating the piece once more, and picking up stitches along the remaining side edge with a fourth needle. Now that you have reached the first group of live stitches, you can place a marker and knit in the round using a fifth needle (if you are using DPNs). If you are using a circular needle, place a marker and proceed to knit the stitches in the round.

Embroidery

Want to give your toy a mouth, whiskers, eyebrows, or other embellishments? Embroidering details onto your knitting with contrasting-colored yarn will add lots of personality.

Back Stitch

Back stitch is the best way to embroider a curved or straight line on your knitting.

❶ Start by making your first stitch, and bring the needle out where you want the second stitch to start.

❷ Pull the yarn through, then insert the needle in the same place where you inserted it for the first stitch.

❸ After repeating Steps 1 and 2 several times, you will have a line of stitches with no gaps between them. When stitching a curved line, remember to bring your needle out where you want your next stitch to end.

Duplicate Stitch

Duplicate stitch is a handy technique that gives the illusion of a change in color within the knitted fabric without having to actually knit the new color.

1 Bring the needle out from the middle of a stitch, just under the downward point of the stitch's V. Then insert your needle horizontally under the V immediately above.

2 Insert the needle into the same place that you started to form one stitch. To make another duplicate stitch above the one you just made, bring the needle back out immediately above the place where you just inserted it.

3 The result is a stitch that "duplicates" the knitted stitch beneath it in a new color. Repeat Steps 1–2 for each stitch.

The animal kingdom has some huge new rulers! They're instituting a cute-ocracy, so we can anticipate a wildly adorable new era.

Colossal

Critters

Roary

A baby dinosaur with a bratty attitude, Roary dishes out raspberries instead of dino bites. Give his belly a big squeeze and you'll be BFFs again. Just don't tease him about his extinct uncle.

BODY

Base

With A, cast on 4 stitches onto one DPN.

Rnd 1 (work as I-cord): [Kfb] 4 times (8 sts).

Distribute stitches onto 3 needles to continue working in a round.

Rnd 2: [Kfb] 8 times (16 sts).

Rnd 3: Knit.

Rnd 4: [Kfb, k1] 8 times (24 sts).

Rnd 5: Knit.

Rnd 6: [Kfb, k2] 8 times (32 sts).

Rnd 7: Knit.

Rnds 8–22: Continue to increase 8 stitches every other round, with the number of knit stitches after the kfb increasing by 1 each time, until there are 96 stitches on the needle. Along the way, switch to the circular needle whenever it's more comfortable.

Belly

You will now incorporate B and work this section flat, turning after every row. You will also incorporate the second skein of A as noted. (See Belly chart on page 40 for a visual guide to Rows 1–26.)

Note: When switching colors, twist the old color once around the new color on the backside of the piece before working the first stitch in the new color. (See Intarsia Color Change on page 150.)

Row 1: K44A (from original skein), k8B, k44A (from skein 2).

Row 2: P42A (from skein 2), p12B, p42A (from original skein).

Continue to use the original skein of A for one section, and skein 2 for the other section.

Row 3: K40A, k16B, k40A.

Row 4: P39A, p1B, k16B, p1B, p39A.

Row 5: K38A, k20B, k38A.

Row 6: P38A, p20B, p38A.

Row 7: K37A, k22B, k37A.

Row 8: P37A, p1B, k20B, p1B, p37A.

Row 9: K37A, k22B, k37A.

Row 10: P37A, p22B, p37A.

Rows 11–18: Repeat Rows 7–10 twice more.

Row 19: K37A, k22B, k37A.

Row 20: P37A, p1B, k20B, p1B, p37A.

Row 21: K38A, k20B, k38A.

Row 22: P38A, p20B, p38A.

Row 23: K39A, k18B, k39A.

Row 24: P40A, p1B, k14B, p1B, p40A.

Row 25: K42A, k12B, k42A.

Row 26: P44A, p8B, p44A.

Mouth and Top of Head

Break B and the second skein of A, and continue with original skein of A only.

Row 1: Knit.

Instead of turning for the next row, rejoin into a round.

Rnds 2–5: Knit (4 rnds).

Rnd 6: K43, bind off 10 stitches (begin binding off with sts 44 and 45), k to end (86 sts).

Rnds 7–8: K43, then turn and purl. Keep purling past the beginning of the round, and continue until you reach the bound-off stitches from Round 6. Turn again, and knit to the end of the round.

Rnd 9: K43, cast on 10 stitches using backward loop method, k to end (96 sts).

Rnds 10–15: Knit (6 rnds).

Size
13" (33cm) tall

Skill Level
Intermediate

Techniques
Intarsia (page 150), backward-loop cast-on (page 148), mattress stitch (page 28)

Yarn
Bulky yarn in 4 colors, plus small amount of contrasting color

Sample knit with Cascade 128 Superwash, 100% wool, 3½ oz (100g), 128 yds (117m)
2 skeins (256 yds/234m) of 802 Green Apple (A)
1 skein (128 yds/117m) each of:
820 Lemon (B)
1964 Cerise (C)
845 Denim (D)
Less than one skein (128 yds/117m) of 1962 Brown Bear

Needles
Size 8 US (5.0mm) circular needle
Set of size 8 US (5.0mm) double-pointed needles (See Needle Options on page 14)

Other Supplies
One pair of size 18mm safety eyes
Stuffing
Straight pins

Gauge
2" (5cm) = 8 stitches and 12 rows in stockinette stitch (knit on RS, purl on WS)

Rnd 16: [K2tog, k10] 8 times (88 sts).
Rnds 17-20: Knit (4 rnds).
Rnd 21: [K2tog, k9] 8 times (80 sts).
Rnds 22-25: Knit (4 rnds).
Rnd 26: [K2tog, k8] 8 times (72 sts).
Rnds 27 and 28: Knit.
Rnd 29: [K2tog, k7] 8 times (64 sts).
Rnds 30 and 31: Knit.
Rnd 32: [K2tog, k6] 8 times (56 sts).
Rnds 33 and 34: Knit.
Rnd 35: [K2tog, k5] 8 times (48 sts).
Rnd 36: Knit.

Switch to DPNs now or whenever it's comfortable.

Rnds 37-43: Continue to decrease 8 stitches every other round, with the number of knit stitches after the k2tog decreasing by 1 each time, until 16 stitches remain.

Rnd 44: [K2tog] 8 times (8 sts).
Break yarn and draw tightly through the stitches with a tapestry needle.

TONGUE/MOUTH LINING

With C, cast on 26 stitches onto 3 DPNs and join to work in a round.
Rnds 1-10: Knit.
Rnd 11: K2tog, k9, [k2tog] twice, k9, k2tog (22 sts).
Rnd 12: Knit.
Rnd 13: K2tog, k7, [k2tog] twice, k7, k2tog (18 sts).
Rnd 14: Knit.
Rnd 15: K2tog, k5, [k2tog] twice, k5, k2tog (14 sts).
Rnd 16: Knit.

Rnd 17: K2tog, k3, [k2tog] twice, k3, k2tog (10 sts).
Rnd 18: [K2tog] 5 times (5 sts).
Break yarn and draw tightly through the stitches with a tapestry needle.

TAIL

With A, cast on 64 sts onto the circular needle. Making sure not to twist the stitches, place a beginning-of-round marker and join in a round.
Rnds 1-10: Knit.
Rnd 11: K16, k2tog, k10, k2tog, k4, k2tog, k10, k2tog, k16 (60 sts).
Rnds 12-15: Knit (4 rnds).
Rnd 16: K15, k2tog, k9, k2tog, k4, k2tog, k9, k2tog, k15 (56 sts).

Belly

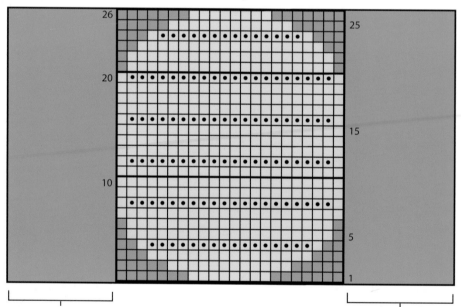

Knit stitches 60-96 on odd-numbered rows
Purl stitches 1-37 on even-numbered rows

Knit stitches 1-37 on odd-numbered rows
Purl stitches 60-96 on even-numbered rows

■ Knit with A on odd-numbered rows, purl with A on even-numbered rows
Note: Work with original skein of A for the stitches on the right half of the chart, and with Skein 2 of A for the stitches on the left half of the chart.

□ Knit with B on odd-numbered rows, purl with B on even-numbered rows
⊡ Knit with B (always on even-numbered rows)

Rnds 17 and 18: Knit.

Rnd 19: K14, k2tog, k8, k2tog, k4, k2tog, k8, k2tog, k14 (52 sts).

Rnd 20: Knit.

Rnd 21: K13, k2tog, k7, k2tog, k4, k2tog, k7, k2tog, k13 (48 sts).

Rnd 22: Knit.

Rnd 23: K12, k2tog, k6, k2tog, k4, k2tog, k6, k2tog, k12 (44 sts).

Rnd 24: Knit.

Rnd 25: K11, k2tog, k5, k2tog, k4, k2tog, k5, k2tog, k11 (40 sts).

Rnds 26 and 27: Knit.

Rnd 28: K10, k2tog, k4, k2tog, k4, k2tog, k4, k2tog, k10 (36 sts).

Rnds 29 and 30: Knit.

Rnd 31: K9, k2tog, k3, k2tog, k4, k2tog, k3, k2tog, k9 (32 sts).

Rnds 32–35: Knit (4 rnds).

Rnd 36: K8, k2tog, k2, k2tog, k4, k2tog, k2, k2tog, k8 (28 sts).

Rnds 37–40: Knit (4 rnds).

Rnd 41: K7, k2tog, k1, k2tog, k4, k2tog, k1, k2tog, k7 (24 sts).

Rnds 42–45: Knit (4 rnds).

Rnd 46: K5, k2tog, k2, k2tog, k2, k2tog, k2, k2tog, k5 (20 sts).

Rnds 47 and 48: Knit.

Rnd 49: K4, k2tog, k1, k2tog, k2, k2tog, k1, k2tog, k4 (16 sts).

Rnds 50 and 51: Knit.

Rnd 52: K3, [k2tog] twice, k2, [k2tog] twice, k3 (12 sts).

Rnds 53 and 54: Knit.

Rnd 55: [K2tog] 6 times (6 sts).

Break yarn and draw tightly through the stitches with a tapestry needle.

ARMS (make 2)

With A, cast on 6 stitches onto 3 DPNs and join to work in a round.

Rnd 1: [Kfb] 6 times (12 sts).

Rnds 2–9: Knit (8 rnds).

Rnd 10: Kfb, k4, [kfb] twice, k4, kfb (16 sts).

Rnd 11: Knit.

Rnd 12: Kfb, k6, [kfb] twice, k6, kfb (20 sts).

Rnds 13–16: Knit (4 rnds).

Rnd 17: K2tog, k6, [k2tog] twice, k6, k2tog (16 sts).

Rnd 18: Knit.

Rnd 19: K2tog, k4, [k2tog] twice, k4, k2tog (12 sts).

Stuff piece.

Rnd 20: [K2tog] 6 times (6 sts).

Break yarn and draw tightly through the stitches with a tapestry needle.

Pull my mouth inside out to make my tongue stick out.

Nyah!

LEGS (make 2)

With A, cast on 6 stitches onto 3 DPNs and join to work in a round.
Rnd 1: [Kfb] 6 times (12 sts).
Rnds 2–13: Knit (12 rnds).
Rnd 14: Kfb, k4, [kfb] twice, k4, kfb (16 sts).
Rnd 15: Knit.
Rnd 16: Kfb, k6, [kfb] twice, k6, kfb (20 sts).
Rnds 17–24: Knit (8 rnds).
Rnd 25: K2tog, k6, [k2tog] twice, k6, k2tog (16 sts).
Rnd 26: Knit.
Rnd 27: K2tog, k4, [k2tog] twice, k4, k2tog (12 sts).
    Stuff piece.
Rnd 28: [K2tog] 6 times (6 sts).
    Break yarn and draw tightly through the stitches with a tapestry needle.

SPIKES (make 2 each in B, C, and D)

Cast on 20 stitches onto 3 DPNs and join to work in a round.
Rnds 1–3: Knit.
Rnd 4: K2tog, k6, [k2tog] twice, k6, k2tog (16 sts).
Rnds 5 and 6: Knit.
Rnd 7: K2tog, k4, [k2tog] twice, k4, k2tog (12 sts).
Rnds 8 and 9: Knit.
Rnd 10: K2tog, k2, [k2tog] twice, k2, k2tog (8 sts).
Rnd 11: Knit.
Rnd 12: [K2tog] 4 times (4 sts).
    Break yarn and draw tightly through the stitches with a tapestry needle.

FINISHING

Stuff the body, and stitch together the vertical opening at back using mattress stitch.

Attach the eyes above and to either side of the mouth hole, spaced 12 stitches apart.

Turn the tongue/mouth lining purl side out, and insert into the mouth opening. Line up the cast-on edges of the piece with the cast-on/bound-off edges of the opening, and stitch the lining to the mouth using mattress stitch. (Even though the lining is purl side out, the tapestry needle should go under the knit stitches on the inside.) Before closing up the seam, make sure you are happy with the amount of stuffing in the body—it should be fully filled out, but also able to accommodate the concave mouth.

With a contrasting color, embroider two nostrils onto the face with 2 small horizontal stitches for each, placed 3 stitches above the mouth and spaced 1½ stitches apart.

Stuff the tail, and hold it so that the beginning of the rounds points down, and the mid-round section of 4 straight stitches points up. Pin the top of the tail's cast-on edge to the middle back of the body, just above the seam you closed up. Pin the bottom side of the cast-on edge directly below the seam, on the third-to-last increase round on

the body. Add more pins around the cast-on edge, so that it forms a circle on the body.

Beginning at the bottom of the tail, attach the tail to the body using mattress stitch, removing the pins as you come to them. Before completing the seam, add more stuffing to the tail to fill it out.

Stuff the arms, and attach their cast-on edges to the sides of the body using mattress stitch, with each placed about 12 stitches outside the belly, and about 5 stitches above it.

Stuff the legs. Fold the bigger part upward and stitch in place for upward-turned feet. Attach the cast-on edge of each one just below and to the outside of the belly.

Lay the spikes flat, then stuff and seam the cast-on edges together using mattress stitch. Pin the spikes to the body and tail, each spaced approximately 6 stitches apart. Once you are happy with the placement, attach the underside of each spike to the body or tail using one straight row of stitches. (If you pull the stitches tightly enough, the spike should stand upright, but if they are floppy, you can stitch around the base of each spike on both sides.)

Weave in loose ends.

Switch to A (and break C and B).

Rnds 25–28: Knit 4 rounds.

Rnd 29: [K2tog, k2] 8 times (24 sts).

Rnds 30 and 31: Knit.

Rnd 32: [K2tog, k1] 8 times (16 sts).

Rnd 33: Knit.

Stuff the piece about one-quarter full, so that when you fold the first half of the piece up into the second half, it appears filled out and has a hollow underside.

Attach 12mm eyes, placed 2 stitches below first decrease round and spaced 7 stitches apart.

Rnd 34: [K2tog] 8 times (8 sts).

Break yarn and draw tightly through the stitches with a tapestry needle.

Beak

With F, cast on 3 stitches onto one DPN.

Knit 1 round of I-cord, then break yarn and draw tightly through stitches with a tapestry needle.

Wings (make 2)

With A, cast on 4 stitches onto one DPN to work flat.

Row 1: Purl.

Row 2: [K2tog] twice (2 sts).

Break yarn and draw tightly through the stitches with a tapestry needle.

Finishing

Fold the bottom half of the body up into the top half, massaging the stuffing so that the body is filled out and has a hollow underside.

Attach the cast-on edge of the beak to the body using mattress stitch, placed between and just below the eyes.

Attach the wings knit side up to the sides of the body using mattress stitch, placed 2 stitches below the last color change, and just behind each eye.

Weave in loose ends.

Or our fashion sense!

The von Trapp family's got nothing on our harmonizing!

MEDIUM BIRD

Body

With A, cast on 8 stitches onto 3 DPNs and join to work in a round.

Rnd 1: [Kfb] 8 times (16 sts).

Rnd 2: Knit.

Rnd 3: [Kfb, k1] 8 times (24 sts).

Rnd 4: Knit.

Rnd 5: [Kfb, k2] 8 times (32 sts).

Rnd 6: Knit.

Rnd 7: [Kfb, k7] 4 times (36 sts).

Rnds 8–21: Knit (14 rnds).

Rnd 22: [Kfb, k8] 4 times (40 sts).

Rnd 23: Knit.

Rnd 24: [Kfb, k4] 8 times (48 sts).

Rnds 25 and 26: Knit.

Rnd 27: [Kfb, k5] 8 times (56 sts).

Transfer stitches to the circular needle now, or whenever it's comfortable.

Switch to D (and break A).

Rnd 28: Knit.

Rnds 29–40: Work according to the Medium Bird chart (page 48), incorporating B, for 12 rounds.

Switch to A (and break D and B).

Rnds 41–46: Knit (6 rnds).

Rnd 47: [K2tog, k5] 8 times (48 sts).

Rnds 48 and 49: Knit.

Transfer stitches to DPNs now, or whenever it's comfortable.

Rnd 50: [K2tog, k4] 8 times (40 sts).

Rnds 51 and 52: Knit.

Rnd 53: [K2tog, k3] 8 times (32 sts).

Rnd 54: Knit.

Rnd 55: [K2tog, k2] 8 times (24 sts).

Rnd 56: Knit.

Stuff the piece about one-quarter full, so that when you fold the first half of the piece up into the second half, it appears filled out and has a hollow underside.

Attach 15mm eyes, placed one stitch below the first decrease round, and spaced 12 stitches apart.

Rnd 57: [K2tog, k1] 8 times (16 sts).

Rnd 58: [K2tog] 8 times.

Break yarn and draw tightly through the stitches with a tapestry needle.

Beak

With F, cast on 6 stitches onto 3 DPNs and join to work in a round.

Knit 2 rounds.

Break yarn and draw tightly through the stitches with a tapestry needle.

Wings (make 2)

With A, cast on 6 stitches onto 1 DPN to work flat.

Row 1: K1, kfb, k2, kfb, k1 (8 sts).

Rows 2, 4, and 6: Purl.

Row 3: Knit.

Row 5: K1, k2tog, k2 k2tog, k1 (6 sts).

Row 7: [K2tog] 3 times (3 sts).

Break yarn and draw tightly through the stitches with a tapestry needle.

Finishing

Fold the bottom half of the body up into the top half, massaging the stuffing so that the body is filled out and has a hollow underside.

Without stuffing the beak, attach the cast-on edge to the body using mattress stitch, placed between and just below the eyes.

Attach the wings knit side up to the sides of the body using mattress stitch, placed 3 stitches below the last color change, and 6 stitches back from each eye.

Weave in loose ends.

LARGE BIRD

Body

With A, cast on 8 stitches onto 3 DPNs and join to work in a round.

Rnd 1: [Kfb] 8 times (16 sts).

Rnd 2: [Kfb, k1] 8 times (24 sts).

Rnd 3: Knit.

Rnd 4: [Kfb, k2] 8 times (32 sts).

Rnd 5: Knit.

Rnd 6: [Kfb, k3] 8 times (40 sts).

Rnd 7: Knit.

Rnd 8: [Kfb, k4] 8 times (48 sts).

Rnds 9 and 10: Knit.

Rnd 11: [Kfb, k5] 8 times (56 sts).

Transfer stitches to the circular needle now, or whenever it's comfortable.

Rnds 12 and 13: Knit.

Rnd 14: [Kfb, k13] 4 times (60 sts).

Rnds 15–36: Knit (22 rounds).

Rnd 37: [Kfb, k14] 4 times (64 sts).

Rnd 38: [Kfb, k7] 8 times (72 sts).

Rnd 39: Knit.

Rnd 40: [Kfb, k8] 8 times (80 sts).

Rnds 41–43: Knit (3 rnds).

Rnd 44: [Kfb, k9] 8 times (88 sts).

Switch to E (and break A).

Rnd 45: Knit.

Rnds 46–63: Work according to the Large Bird chart (page 48), incorporating B, for 18 rounds.

Rnd 64: Knit with E only.

Switch to A (and break E and B).

Rnds 65–70: Knit (6 rnds).

Rnd 71: [K2tog, k9] 8 times (80 sts).
Rnds 72–75: Knit (4 rnds).
Rnd 76: [K2tog, k8] 8 times (72 sts).
Rnds 77 and 78: Knit.
Rnd 79: [K2tog, k7] 8 times (64 sts).
Rnds 80 and 81: Knit.
Rnd 82: [K2tog, k6] 8 times (56 sts).
Rnds 83 and 84: Knit.
Rnd 85: [K2tog, k5] 8 times (48 sts).
    Transfer stitches to DPNs now, or whenever it's comfortable.
Rnd 86: Knit.
Rnd 87: [K2tog, k4] 8 times (40 sts).
Rnd 88: Knit.
Rnd 89: [K2tog, k3] 8 times (32 sts).
Rnd 90: Knit.
    Stuff piece about one-third full, so that when you fold the first half of the piece up into the second half, it appears filled out and has a hollow underside.
    Attach 18mm eyes, placed one stitch below the second decrease round, and spaced 16 stitches apart.
Rnd 91: [K2tog, k2] 8 times (24 sts).
Rnd 92: Knit.

Rnd 93: [K2tog, k1] 8 times (16 sts).
Rnd 94: [K2tog] 8 times (8 sts).
    Break yarn and draw tightly through the stitches with a tapestry needle.

Beak
With F, cast on 9 stitches onto 3 DPNs and join to work in a round.
Rnds 1–4: Knit.
Rnd 5: [K2tog, k1] 3 times (6 sts).
    Break yarn and draw tightly through the stitches with a tapestry needle.

Wings (make 2)
With A, cast on 8 stitches onto one DPN to work flat.
Row 1 and all odd-numbered rows through Row 11: Purl.
Row 2: K1, kfb, k4, kfb, k1 (10 sts).
Row 4: K1, kfb, k6, kfb, k1 (12 sts).
Row 6: Knit.
Row 8: K1, k2tog, k6, k2tog, k1 (10 sts).
Row 10: K1 k2tog, k4, k2tog, k1 (8 sts).
Row 12: K1, k2tog, k2, k2tog, k1 (6 sts).
Row 13: [P2tog] 3 times (3 sts).
    Bind off all stitches.

Finishing
Fold the bottom half of the body up into the top half, massaging the stuffing so that the body is filled out and has a hollow underside.
    Stuff beak, and attach the cast-on edge to the body using mattress stitch, placed between and just below the eyes.
    Attach the wings knit side up to the sides of the body using mattress stitch, placed 4 stitches below the last color change, and 6 stitches back from each eye.
    Weave in loose ends.

Medium Bird

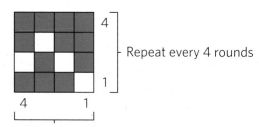

4 — Repeat every 4 rounds — 1

4 — 1

Repeat every 4 stitches in the round

Knit with D   Knit with B

Large Bird

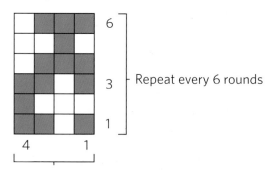

6

3 — Repeat every 6 rounds

1

4 — 1

Repeat every 4 stitches in the round

Knit with E   Knit with B

Stuff piece fully, without overstuffing.

Attach the larger eyes 2 stitches down from the first decrease round on the head, centered above the tummy bulge you made in Rounds 19–28, and spaced 15 stitches apart.

Rnd 99: [K2tog, k2] 8 times (24 sts).
Rnd 100: Knit.
Rnd 101: [K2tog, k1] 8 times (16 sts).
Rnd 102: [K2tog] 8 times (8 sts).

Break yarn and draw tightly through the stitches with a tapestry needle.

Muzzle

With B, cast on 32 stitches onto 3 DPNs and join in a round.
Rnds 1 and 2: Knit.
Rnd 3: [K2tog, k2] 8 times (24 sts).
Rnds 4 and 5: Knit.
Rnd 6: [K2tog, k1] 8 times (16 sts).
Rnd 7: Knit.
Rnd 8: [K2tog] 8 times (8 sts).

Break yarn and draw tightly through the stitches with a tapestry needle.

Ears (make 2)

With A, cast on 30 stitches onto 3 DPNs, leaving a tail for attaching, and join in a round.

Rnds 1–6: Knit.
Rnd 7: K2tog, k11, [k2tog] twice, k11, k2tog (26 sts).
Rnd 8: Knit.
Rnd 9: K2tog, k9, [k2tog] twice, k9, k2tog (22 sts).
Rnd 10: Knit.
Rnd 11: [K2tog] twice, k3, [k2tog] 4 times, k3, [k2tog] twice (14 sts).
Rnd 12: [K2tog] 7 times (7 sts).

Break yarn and draw tightly through the stitches with a tapestry needle.

Ear Patches (make 2)

With B, cast on 12 stitches onto one DPN to work flat.
Row 1: Purl.
Row 2: Knit.
Row 3: Purl.
Row 4: K1, k2tog, k6, ssk, k1 (10 sts).
Row 5: Purl.
Row 6: K1, [k2tog] twice, [ssk] twice, k1 (6 sts).
Row 7: Purl.

Bind off all stitches.

Arms (make 2)

With A, cast on 6 stitches onto 3 DPNs, leaving a tail for attaching, and join in a round.
Rnd 1: [Kfb] 6 times (12 sts).
Rnd 2: [Kfb, k1] 6 times (18 sts).
Rnd 3: Knit.
Rnd 4: [Kfb, k2] 6 times (24 sts).
Rnds 5–30: Knit (26 rnds).

Who needs fur when you can wear a sweater?

Rnd 31: [K2tog, k2] 6 times (18 sts).

Rnd 32: Knit.

Rnd 33: [K2tog, k1] 6 times (12 sts).
  Stuff piece.

Rnd 34: [K2tog] 6 times.
  Break yarn and draw tightly through the stitches with a tapestry needle.

Arm Pads (make 2)

With B, cast on 6 stitches onto 1 DPN to work flat.

Row 1: Purl.

Row 2: K1, kfb, k2, kfb, k1 (8 sts).

Row 3: Purl.

Row 4: Knit.

Row 5: Purl.

Row 6: K1, k2tog, k2, ssk, k1 (6 sts).

Row 7: Purl.
  Bind off all stitches.

Legs (make 2)

With A, cast on 6 stitches onto 3 DPNs, leaving a 10" (25.5cm) tail for attaching, and join in a round.

Rnd 1: [Kfb] 6 times (12 sts).

Rnd 2: [Kfb, k1] 6 times (18 sts).

Rnd 3: Knit.

Rnd 4: [Kfb, k2] 6 times (24 sts).

Rnds 5–20: Knit (16 rnds).

Rnd 21: K18, w+t, p17, w+t, k16, w+t, p15, w+t, k14, w+t, p13, w+t, k12, w+t, p11, w+t, k10, w+t, p9, w+t, k8, w+t, p7, w+t, k to end.

Rnds 22–31: Knit 10 rounds on all 24 sts, picking up the wraps in the first round.

Rnd 32: [K2tog, k2] 6 times (18 sts).

Rnd 33: Knit.

Rnd 34: [K2tog, k1] 6 times (12 sts).
  Stuff piece.

Rnd 35: [K2tog] 6 times (6 sts).
  Break yarn and draw tightly through the stitches with a tapestry needle.

Leg Pads (make 2)

With B, cast on 6 stitches onto one DPN to work flat.

Row 1: Purl.

Row 2: K1, kfb, k2, kfb, k1 (8 sts).

Rows 3–9: Work 7 rows of stockinette stitch.

Row 10: K1, k2tog, k2, ssk, k1 (6 sts).

Row 11: Purl.
  Bind off all stitches.

Tail

With A, cast on 6 stitches onto 3 DPNs, leaving a tail for attaching, and join in a round.

Rnd 1: [Kfb] 6 times (12 sts).

Rnds 2 and 3: Knit.

Rnd 4: Kfb, k4, [kfb] twice, k4, kfb (16 sts).

Rnds 5–8: Knit (4 rnds).
  Stuff piece.

Rnd 9: [K2tog] 8 times (8 sts).
  Break yarn and draw tightly through the stitches with a tapestry needle.

Finishing

All of the following seaming and attaching should be done using mattress stitch.

  Pin the cast-on edge of the muzzle to the face between the eyes, with the top of the muzzle aligned halfway up the eyes.

  Attach the muzzle to the face, stuffing the piece lightly before finishing the seam.

  With C, embroider a nose onto the center of the muzzle with 5 horizontal stitches.

  Use the tails you left on the ears, arms, legs, and tail to attach each to the body.

  Flatten the ears along the decrease "seams," lightly stuff them, and attach them to the sides of the head, placed 8 stitches down from the top of the head and 9 stitches back from each eye.

  Attach the arms to the body at a downward angle, placed directly below the ears and just under the last decrease round on the belly.

  Attach the legs to the underside of the body, 12 rounds up from the beginning of the piece and spaced 16 stitches apart. Make sure that the toes are pointing up when you attach them.

  Place an ear patch against the front of the ear, and use mattress stitch to seam the edges of the patch neatly to the ear. Repeat with the other ear patch.

  Attach the arm pads to the "palms" of the paws (the sections of the arms close to the end, and angled slightly out from the body).

  Do the same with the leg pads, stitching them to the sole of each foot.

  Attach the tail to the back of the body 5 stitches up from the last increase round on the backside.

  Weave in loose ends.

SWEATER (worked bottom to top)

Body

With D, cast on 100 stitches onto the circular needle and join in a round.

Rnds 1–3: [K1, p1] to end.

Rnd 4: Knit.

Rnd 5: K50, pm, k50.

Rnd 6: [K2tog] twice, k to 4 sts before marker, [ssk] twice, sm, [k2tog] twice, k to last 4 sts, [ssk] twice (92 sts).

Rnds 7 and 8: Knit.

Rnd 9: Work same as Round 6 (84 sts).

Rnds 10 and 11: Knit.

Separate Sides

Row 12: K1, [k2tog] twice, k32 (to 5 sts before marker), [ssk] twice, k1 (38 sts).

Place the remaining 42 stitches onto a stitch holder to work later. You will continue working the 38 live stitches flat.

Row 13: Turn, and purl.

Row 14: K1, [k2tog] twice, k28, [ssk] twice, k1 (34 sts).

Row 15: Purl.

Row 16: K1, k2tog, k28, ssk, k1 (32 sts).

Row 17: Purl.

Row 18: Knit.

Row 19: Purl.

Row 20: K1, [kfb] twice, k26, [kfb] twice, k1 (36 sts).

Row 21: Bind off 2 stitches, leaving one stitch on the right end of the needle and 33 on the left. [P1, k1] to last 3 stitches, k3 (34 sts).

Row 22: Bind off 2 stitches, leaving one stitch on the right end of the needle and 31 on the left. [P1, k1] to end (32 sts).

Place the 42 held stitches onto the circular needle, and place the 32 stitches you just worked onto the holder.

Break yarn, and reattach it to the first stitch on the needle.

Repeat Rows 12–22 with these stitches.

Rejoin Sides

Leave the yarn attached—the last stitch you just worked will again become the last stitch in the round. Place the 32 held stitches onto the circular needle to rejoin the 64 stitches in a round.

Rnds 1–6: [K1, p1] to end.

Bind off as established.

Sleeves (make 2)

With D, cast on 24 sts onto 3 DPNs, leaving a tail for seaming, and join in a round.

Rnd 1: Knit.

Rnd 2: Kfb, k to last st, kfb (26 sts).

Rnds 3–22: Knit (20 rnds).

Rnds 23 and 24: [K1, p1] to end.

Bind off as established.

Finishing

Using the tails you left on the sleeves, stitch the sleeves into the armholes, beginning at the armhole center bottom.

Weave in loose ends, then block the sweater by dampening it and laying it flat to dry. Fold the top ribbing halfway down, as you do for a rolled-down turtleneck look.

THEO

Body and Head (worked bottom to top)

With A, cast on 4 stitches onto one DPN.

Rnd 1 (work as I-cord): [Kfb] 4 times (8 sts).

Distribute stitches onto 3 needles to continue working in a round.

Rnd 2: [Kfb] 8 times (16 sts).

Rnd 3: Knit.

Rnd 4: [Kfb, k1] 8 times (24 sts).

Rnd 5: Knit.

Rnd 6: K1, kfb, k8, kfb, k2, kfb, k8, kfb, k1 (28 sts).

Rnd 7: Knit.

Rnd 8: K1, kfb, k10, kfb, k2, kfb, k10, kfb, k1 (32 sts).

Rnds 9–16: Knit (8 rnds).

Rnd 17: [K2tog, k2] 8 times (24 sts).

Rnds 18 and 19: Knit.

Rnd 20: [K2tog, k1] 8 times (16 sts).

Rnd 21: [Kfb, k1] 8 times (24 sts).

Rnds 22 and 23: Knit.

Rnd 24: [Kfb, k2] 8 times (32 sts).

Rnds 25–31: Knit (7 rnds).

Rnd 32: [K2tog, k2] 8 times (24 sts).

Rnds 33 and 34: Knit.

Rnd 35: [K2tog, k1] 8 times (16 sts).

Rnd 36: Knit.

Stuff piece and attach smaller eyes, placed one stitch below the first decrease round on the face, and spaced 5 stitches apart.

Rnd 37: [K2tog] 8 times (8 sts).

Break yarn and draw tightly through the stitches with a tapestry needle.

Ears (make 2)

With A, cast on 12 stitches onto 3 DPNs, leaving a tail for attaching, and join in a round.

Rnds 1 and 2: Knit.

Rnd 3: [K2tog] 6 times (6 sts).

Break yarn and draw tightly through the stitches with a tapestry needle.

Arms/Legs (make 4)

With A, cast on 4 stitches onto one DPN, leaving a tail for attaching.

Rnd 1 (work as I-cord): [Kfb] 4 times (8 sts).

Distribute stitches onto 3 needles to continue working in a round.

Rnds 2–7: Knit (6 rnds).

Switch to B.

Rnd 8: Knit.

Stuff piece. Break yarn and draw tightly through the stitches with a tapestry needle.

Finishing

With C, embroider the nose onto the face with 3 stitches between and just below the eyes.

Using the tails you left on the ears, arms, and legs, attach each to the body using mattress stitch.

Flatten the ears along the decrease stitches, and attach them 2 stitches down from the top of the head, and 4 stitches back from each eye.

Attach arms at a downward angle, directly beneath the ears and just below the last decrease round on the belly.

Attach the legs 4 rounds up from the beginning of the piece, and spaced 4 stitches apart.

With B, embroider patches onto the ears with 4 horizontal stitches.

For the tail, turn the body around and upside down, and pick up and knit 2 stitches at the back of the body, just above the last increase round on the base.

Row 1 (work as I-cord): [Kfb] twice.

Row 2 (work as I-cord): Knit.

Break yarn and draw tightly through the stitches with a tapestry needle.

Weave in loose ends.

SCARF

With D, cast on 4 stitches onto one DPN to work flat.

Knit every row until the piece is 13" (33cm) long, or long enough to wrap around the bear's neck with some extra on each end.

Bind off all stitches.

Cut six 4" (10cm) strands of D. Fold each in half and attach to the end of the scarf by pulling the folded loop through the scarf with a crochet hook (A, below) and then pulling the ends through the loop and tightening (B, below). Trim ends.

A. To make a tassel on the scarf, fold a strand of yarn in half, and pull the loop through the scarf with a crochet hook.

B. Pull the ends through the loop and tighten.

Squidpocalypse

A giant squid friend will clean out your gutters and fetch lost grapes from under the fridge. He's handy to have around—literally! Just don't make the mistake of lending him your car keys. Everyone knows that squids are terrible drivers.

BODY (worked from the tips of the arms up in one piece)

Arms (make 8)

Setup

With A, cast on 6 stitches onto 3 DPNs and join to work in a round.

Rnd 1: [Kfb] 6 times (12 sts).

Rnd 2: Knit.

Rnd 3: [Kfb, k1] 6 times (18 sts).

Repeated Pattern

You will next incorporate B and switch to flat knitting. Place the stitches onto one DPN when it's more comfortable than 3.

Note: When switching colors, twist the old color once around the new color on the purl side before working the second stitch in the new color.

Row 1: K9A, k9B. Turn.

Row 2: P9B, p9A.

Row 3: K9A, then with B, k2, bobble1, k6. (See box, at right.)

Row 4: P9B, p9A.

Row 5: K9A, k9B.

Row 6: P9B, p9A.

Row 7: K9A, then with B, k5, bobble1, k3.

Row 8: P9B, p9A.

Repeat Rows 1–8 until there are 2 columns of 11 bobbles each.

Work Rows 1–7 once more, so that you have 12 bobbles in each column.

Without turning for a purl row, break the yarns and divide the two colored sections onto 2 DPNs. Place the 9 B stitches from right to left onto the circular needle, and thread the 9 A stitches from left to right onto to a 12" (30.5cm) strand of waste yarn.

Make 8 arms total, placing the B and A stitches of each arm onto the circular needle and the waste yarn, respectively, so that they can be neatly laid out side by side. Don't break the B yarn on the last arm. When you place the last arm onto the needle, the working yarn should be attached to the leftmost stitch on the knit side (A, page 58).

Tie the ends of the waste yarn together, and curve the needle so that the 8 arms form a circle.

Bobble1

Knit into the front and back of the stitch 3 times (making 6 stitches on the right needle), then pass the first 5 increase stitches over the last stitch on the right needle.

Size

Main body section is 17" (43cm) long; arms are each 18" (45.5cm) long; full body from top to longest tentacle is 47" (119cm) long

Skill Level

Experienced

Techniques

1-row bobble stitch (see box, at left), mattress stitch (page 28), stranded color knitting (page 151)

Yarn

Bulky yarn in 2 colors

Sample knit with Cascade 128 Superwash, 100% wool, 3½ oz (100g) and 128 yds (117m) 5 skeins (640 yds/585m) of 1964 Cerise (A)

3 skeins (384 yds/351m) of 1963 Tutu (B)

Needles

Set of size 8 US (5.0mm) double-pointed needles Size 8 US (5.0mm) circular needle (See Needle Options on page 14)

Other Supplies

Waste yarn
One pair of size 25mm safety eyes
Stuffing

Gauge

2" (5cm) = 8 stitches and 12 rows in stockinette stitch (knit on RS, purl on WS)

Rnd 105: K5, ssk, k20, [ssk] twice, k12, [k2tog] twice, k20, k2tog, k5 (68 sts).
Rnd 106: Knit.
Rnd 107: K5, ssk, k18, [ssk] twice, k10, [k2tog] twice, k18, k2tog, k5 (62 sts).
Rnd 108: Knit.
Rnd 109: K5, ssk, k16, [ssk] twice, k8, [k2tog] twice, k16, k2tog, k5 (56 sts).
Rnd 110: Knit.
Rnd 111: K4, [ssk] twice, k13, [ssk] twice, k6, [k2tog] twice, k13, [k2tog] twice, k4 (48 sts).
 Switch to DPNs now or when it's comfortable.
Rnd 112: Knit.
Rnd 113: K3, [ssk] twice, k11, [ssk] twice, k4, [k2tog] twice, k11, [k2tog] twice, k3 (40 sts).
Rnd 114: Knit.
Rnd 115: [K2tog, k3] 8 times (32 sts).
Rnd 116: Knit.
 Stuff piece, filling it out completely without overstuffing it. Orient the body so that the beginning of the rounds is at the bottom, and attach eyes on either side of the head, placed 4 stitches back from the first decrease round on the head.
Rnd 117: [K2tog, k2] 8 times (24 sts).
Rnd 118: Knit.
Rnd 119: [K2tog, k1] 8 times (16 sts).
Rnd 120: [K2tog] 8 times (8 sts).
 Add a little more stuffing to the end of the piece if necessary, then break yarn and draw tightly through the stitches with a tapestry needle.

Ears (make 2)

With MC, cast on 12 stitches onto 3 DPNs, leaving a tail for seaming, and join to work in a round.
Rnds 1–4: Knit.
Rnd 5: K2tog, k2, [k2tog] twice, k2, k2tog (8 sts).
Rnd 6: Knit.
 Break yarn and draw tightly through the stitches with a tapestry needle.

Legs (make 4)

With MC, cast on 20 stitches onto 3 DPNs, leaving a tail for seaming, and join to work in a round.
Rnds 1–6: Knit.
Rnd 7: K14, w+t, p13, w+t, k12, w+t, p11, w+t, k10, w+t, p9, w+t, k8, w+t, p7, w+t, k6, w+t, p5, w+t, k to end.
Rnds 8–15: Knit (8 rnds).
Rnd 16: [K2tog, k3] 4 times (16 sts).
Rnd 17: [K2tog] 8 times (8 sts).
 Break yarn and draw tightly through the stitches with a tapestry needle.

Tail

With MC, cast on 6 stitches onto 3 DPNs, leaving a tail for seaming, and join to work in a round.
Rnd 1: [Kfb, k1] 3 times (9 sts).
Rnd 2: Knit.
Rnd 3: [Kfb, k2] 3 times (12 sts).
Rnds 4 and 5: Knit.
 Stuff piece.
Rnd 6: [K2tog] 6 times (6 sts).
 Break yarn and draw tightly through the stitches with a tapestry needle.

Nose

With CC, cast on 10 stitches, leaving a tail for seaming, onto one DPN to work flat.
Row 1: Purl.
Row 2: Knit.
Row 3: Purl.
Row 4: K1, k2tog, k4, ssk, k1 (8 sts).
Row 5: Purl.
Row 6: K1, k2tog, k2, ssk, k1 (6 sts).
Row 7: Purl.
Row 8: [K2tog] 3 times (3 sts).
 Bind off all stitches.

Finishing

Using the tails you left on the ears, legs, and tail, attach each to the body with mattress stitch, placed as described below.
 Lightly stuff the ears, and attach them along the 2 increase seams at the top of the head.
 Stuff the legs, and with the bent "foot" areas facing forward, attach the front legs just behind the head section of the body, and spaced

Why did the capybaras cross the road?

6 stitches apart. Attach the back legs directly behind the front legs, between the third-to-last and second-to-last increase rounds on the body.

Attach the tail just above the cast-on stitches on the body.

Place the nose on the front of the head, with the cast-on edge pointed up and aligned with the closed-up end of the body. Use mattress stitch around the edges of the nose to attach it to the body. With CC, embroider one vertical stitch below the nose.

Weave in loose ends.

BABY CAPYBARA

Body and Head (worked back to front)

With MC, cast on 4 stitches onto 3 DPNs and join to work in a round.
Rnd 1 (work as I-cord): [Kfb] 4 times (8 sts).

Distribute stitches onto 3 needles to continue working in a round.
Rnd 2: [Kfb] 8 times (16 sts).
Rnd 3: Knit.
Rnd 4: [Kfb, k1] 8 times (24 sts).
Rnd 5: Knit.
Rnd 6: [Kfb, k2] 8 times (32 sts).
Rnds 7 and 8: Knit.
Rnd 9: [Kfb, k3] 8 times (40 sts).
Rnds 10–21: Knit (12 rnds).
Rnd 22: [K2tog, k3] 8 times (32 sts).
Rnds 23 and 24: Knit.
Rnd 25: [K2tog, k2] 8 times (24 sts).
Rnd 26: Knit.
Rnd 27: [Kfb, k2] 8 times (32 sts).
Rnd 28: Knit.
Rnd 29: [Kfb, k7] 4 times (36 sts).
Rnds 30–37: Knit (8 rnds).
Rnd 38: [K2tog, k7] 4 times (32 sts).
Rnd 39: Knit.
Rnd 40: [K2tog, k2] 8 times (24 sts).
Rnd 41: Knit.

Stuff piece and attach eyes on either side of head, placed 4 stitches up from the last increase round on the head.
Rnd 42: [K2tog, k1] 8 times (16 sts).
Rnd 43: Knit.

Rnd 44: [K2tog] 8 times (8 sts).
Break yarn and draw tightly through the stitches with a tapestry needle.

Ears (make 2)
With MC, cast on 6 stitches onto 3 DPNs, leaving a tail for seaming, and join to work in a round.

Knit 3 rounds.

Break yarn and draw tightly through the stitches with a tapestry needle.

Legs (make 4)
With MC, cast on 8 stitches onto 3 DPNs, leaving a tail for seaming, and join to work in a round.

Knit 5 rounds.

Break yarn and draw tightly through the stitches with a tapestry needle.

Finishing
Without stuffing them, attach the ears to the head using mattress stitch, each placed 2 stitches behind and to the inside of an eye.

Lightly stuff the legs, and attach to the body using mattress stitch, with the front legs placed just before the increase rounds on the head, and spaced 3 stitches apart, and the back legs placed directly behind the front legs, just above the last increase round on the body.

With CC, embroider the nose with 4–6 horizontal stitches across the closed-up end of the body, and 1 vertical stitch below the horizontal ones.

For the tail, turn the body around, and with MC, pick up and knit 3 stitches with a DPN, just above the cast-on stitches.

Slide the stitches to the right end of the needle, and knit 1 round as an I-cord.

Break yarn and draw tightly through stitches with a tapestry needle.

Weave in loose ends.

Well, somebody's got to be the guinea pig.

It's a little-known fact that knitted capybaras instinctively play follow-the-leader all day long. Great for crossing the street, but it makes for a boring game of tag.

Just because something is little doesn't mean it can't be big. Leave your size-ist assumptions behind, and make your small world larger!

Magnified

Minis

Row 50: Knit.
Row 51: Purl.
Row 52: Knit.
Row 53: Purl.
Row 54: K1, k2tog, k to last 3 sts, k2tog, k1 (38 sts).
Rows 55–118: Repeat Rows 51–54 an additional 16 times (6 sts).
Row 119: Purl.
Row 120: Knit.
Row 121: Purl.
Row 122: K1, [k2tog] twice, k1 (4 sts).

CANDLE

With D, cast on 12 stitches onto 3 DPNs and join to work in a round.
Rnd 1: Knit.
  Switch to E (without breaking D).
Rnds 2 and 3: Knit.
  Switch to D (without breaking E).
Rnds 4 and 5: Knit.

Rnds 6–13: Continue to alternate 2 rounds each of E and D until you have worked 3 stripes of E and 4 stripes of D.
  Stuff piece so far.
  Switch to A.
Rnd 14: [K2tog] 6 times (6 sts).
Rnd 15: [Kfb] 6 times (12 sts).
Rnd 16: [Kfb, k1] 6 times (18 sts).
Rnds 17–20: Knit (4 rnds).
Rnd 21: [K2tog, k1] 6 times (12 sts).
Rnd 22: Knit.
  Stuff the top of the piece.
Rnd 23: [K2tog] 6 times (6 sts).
Rnd 24: Knit.
  Attach eyes, placed 2 stitches up from the last increase round, and spaced 2 stitches apart.
Rnd 25: [K2tog] 3 times (3 sts).
  Break yarn and draw tightly through the stitches with a tapestry needle.

FINISHING

You will complete the cake piece by seaming together the back and top of frosting to the cake's sides and top edges using mattress stitch.

Turn the cake piece so that the frosting is knit side out, and start seaming one edge of the frosting to one side edge of the cake, beginning at the base. The bound-off stitches in Row 48 or 49 of the frosting should align with the top of the C (frosting) area on the cake side. Finish seaming this side, then break the yarn when you reach the top.

Fold the frosting top over the cake, so that the edge facing you aligns with the bound-off edge of the cake side. Note that the side of the frosting should now lie flat against the 5 bound-off stitches from the back area. Seam this side closed.

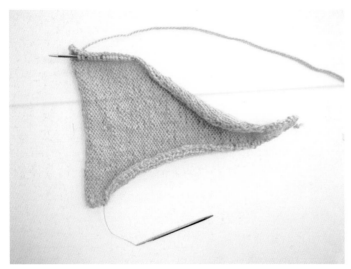

A. After finishing the base, pick up and knit 54 stitches along each of the long sides to begin working the sides of the cake.

B. After working the sides, pick up and knit 50 stitches along the back end of the piece to begin working the frosting.

Next seam the opposite sides of the frosting and cake together, beginning again at the base. Before closing up the seam, stuff the piece fully, and attach the larger eyes to one side of the cake, placed halfway up the section above the stripe of B, and spaced 16 stitches apart.

Place the candle in the middle of the top of the cake, and pin it in place. Use mattress stitch to attach the cast-on edge of the candle to the cake.

Weave in loose ends.

For the frosting embellishment, with C, cast on 3 stitches onto one DPN, and knit an I-cord until it measures 18" (45.5cm) long, or until it's long enough to drape across the back of the piece with 3 dips. Make another I-cord the same length as the first, and pin both in place before attaching with back stitch. (C, at right).

C. *For the frosting embellishment, drape I-cords across the back of the cake and stitch them in place using back stitch.*

Happy birthday to you, happy birthday to you . . .

Oozy & Bristles

These bathroom buddies take "economy size" to the extreme. And there's even more than meets the eye: Give Oozy's paste a tug and he'll spill his guts! Bristles is on cleanup duty, as always.

OOZY

Tube Front

Before starting, divide C into 2 balls of approximately equal size.

With A, cast on 46 stitches onto the circular needle to work flat.

Beginning with a purl row, work 9 rows of stockinette stitch.

Break A.

With B and C, work as shown in Tube Front chart (page 75).

Tube Back

With A, cast on 46 stitches onto the circular needle to work flat.

Beginning with a purl row, work 9 rows of stockinette stitch.

Break A.

With B and C, work as shown in Tube Back chart (page 75).

Break the yarn, and leave the stitches on the needle.

Join Tube/Shape Nozzle

Place the Tube Front stitches onto the working needle alongside the Tube Back stitches, with the working yarn attached to the leftmost stitch on the knit side (64 sts).

Bring the ends of the needle together so that the working yarn is attached to the right end of the needle, and place a marker. You will next work the pieces together into one round.

Switch to A.

Rnds 1 and 2: Knit.

Rnd 3: [K2tog, k6] 8 times (56 sts).

Rnd 4: Knit.

Rnd 5: [K2tog, k5] 8 times (48 sts).

Rnd 6: Knit.

Rnd 7: [K2tog, k4] 8 times (40 sts).

Rnd 8: Knit.

Rnd 9: [K2tog, k3] 8 times (32 sts).

Rnd 10: [K2tog, k6] 4 times (28 sts).

Rnds 11–20: Purl (10 rnds).

Rnd 21: Knit.

Work Lining

Rnd 22: [K2tog, k5] 4 times (24 sts).

Rnds 23–32: Knit (10 rnds).

Rnd 33: [Kfb, k2] 8 times (32 sts).

Rnds 34 and 35: Knit.

Rnd 36: [Kfb, k3] 8 times (40 sts).

Rnds 37 and 38: Knit.

Rnd 39: [Kfb, k4] 8 times (48 sts).

Rnds 40–63: Knit (24 rnds).

Rnd 64: [K2tog, k4] 8 times (40 sts).

Rnd 65: Knit.

Rnd 66: [K2tog, k3] 8 times (32 sts).

Rnd 67: Knit.

Rnd 68: [K2tog, k2] 8 times (24 sts).

Rnd 69: Knit.

Rnd 70: [K2tog, k1] 8 times (16 sts).

Rnd 71: [K2tog] 8 times (8 sts).

Break yarn and draw tightly through the stitches with a tapestry needle.

Paste

With C, cast on 26 stitches onto needle to work flat.

Note: When switching colors in the following rows, twist the old color once around the new color on the backside before working the second stitch in the new color. (See Intarsia Color Change on page 150.)

Sizes
Oozy (toothpaste) is 19" (48.5cm) long (not including paste); Bristles (toothbrush) is 17" (43cm) tall

Skill Level
Experienced

Techniques
Intarsia (page 150), mattress stitch (page 28), picking up stitches on a flat piece (page 149), Kitchener stitch (page 154)

Yarn
Bulky yarn in 6 colors

Samples knit with Knit Picks Brava Bulky, 100% acrylic, 3½ oz (100g), 136 yds (124m) 2 skeins (272 yds/249m) of White (A)
1 skein (136 yds/124m) or less of:
Red (B)
Cornflower (C)
Cream (D)
Rouge (E)
Peapod (F)

Needles
Size 8 US (5.0mm) circular needle
Size 8 US (5.0mm) double-pointed needles
(See Needle Options on page 14)

Other Supplies
1 pair of safety eyes, size 18mm
1 pair of safety eyes, size 25mm
Spare circular needle (size 8 US [5mm] or smaller) or waste yarn
Stuffing

Gauge
2" (5cm) = 7½ stitches and 10 rows in stockinette stitch (knit on RS, purl on WS)

Row 1: K9C, k8D, k9E.
Row 2: P9E, p8D, p9C.
Rows 3–88: Work as established to make a long piece of vertical stripes.
Row 89: K1, [k2tog, k1, k2tog, k1, k2tog] 3 times, k1 (17 sts).
Row 90: Purl.
Row 91: K1, [k2tog, k1, k2tog] 3 times, k1 (11 sts).
Row 92: Purl.
Row 93: K1, [k2tog, k1] 3 times, k1 (8 sts).

Break yarn and draw tightly through the stitches with a tapestry needle from right side to left.

Finishing

Lay tube flat, with the front side on top of the back side, so that the edge stitches line up, with the stripes of C meeting up at the sides.

Beginning at one of the joined ends, seam the two sides together using mattress stitch. Before finishing the last side, attach 25mm eyes, placed as shown, and stuff piece about three-quarters full.

Seam the vertical edges of the paste piece together using mattress stitch, and stuff piece lightly. (It should have volume, but should also be squishy and flexible.)

Stitch the cast-on edges closed, and attach to the closed-up end of the tube lining.

Weave in loose ends.

Stuff the lining and paste into the tube, and pull the paste out for some "messy" fun!

BRISTLES

Handle

With F, cast on 32 sts onto 3 DPNs, place marker, and join to work in a round.
Rnd 1: Knit.
Rnd 2: K1, [kfb] twice, k10, [kfb] twice, k2, [kfb] twice, k10, [kfb] twice, k1 (40 sts).
Rnds 3–62: Knit (60 rnds).
Rnd 63: K1, k2tog, k14, k2tog, k2, k2tog, k14, k2tog, k1 (36 sts).
Rnds 64–66: Knit (3 rnds).
Rnd 67: K1, [kfb] twice, k12, [kfb] twice, k2, [kfb] twice, k12, [kfb] twice, k1 (44 sts).
Rnd 68: Knit.
Rnd 69: K1, kfb, k18, kfb, k2, kfb, k18, kfb, k1 (48 sts).
Rnds 70–99: Knit (30 rnds).
Rnd 100: K1, k2tog, k18, k2tog, k2, k2tog, k18, k2tog, k1 (44 sts).
Rnd 101: Knit.
Rnd 102: K1, [k2tog] twice, k12, [k2tog] twice, k2, [k2tog] twice, k12, [k2tog] twice, k1 (36 sts).
Rnd 103: Knit.
Rnd 104: K1, [k2tog] twice, k8, [k2tog] twice, k2, [k2tog] twice, k8, [k2tog] twice, k1 (28 sts).

Divide stitches into 2 groups of 14 stitches on 2 needles, and bind off using Kitchener stitch (page 154).

Bristles Piece

Increase Stitches

With A, cast on 14 stitches onto one needle to work flat.
Row 1: Purl.
Row 2: K1, kfb, k to last 2 stitches, kfb, k1 (16 sts).
Row 3: Purl.
Row 4: K1, kfb, k to last 2 stitches, kfb, k1 (18 sts).

Work Ridges

For the next 24 rows, work alternating in stockinette stitch every 3 rows.

Row 1: P1, k to last st, p1.
Row 2: K1, p to last st, k1.
Row 3: P1, k to last st, p1.
Row 4: Knit.
Row 5: Purl.
Row 6: Knit

Work Rows 1–6 three more times, for a total of 24 rows.

Work Rows 1–3 once more.

Decrease Stitches

Row 1: K1, k2tog, k to last 3 sts, k2tog, k1 (16 sts).
Row 2: Purl.
Row 3: K1, k2tog, k to last 3 sts, k2tog, k1 (14 sts).
Row 4: Purl.

Work Sides

Instead of turning for the next row, rotate the piece 90 degrees clockwise, and pick up and knit 22 stitches along the adjacent side. Rotate the piece again, and pick up and knit 14 stitches on the cast-on edge. Finally, pick up and knit 22 more stitches along the remaining side (72 sts). Continue to knit the original 14 stitches on the needle, then place a marker. You will now work these stitches in the round. (See Picking Up Stitches around the Perimeter of a Piece, page 33.)

Work 14 rounds in [k1, p1] rib pattern.
Bind off all stitches.

Finishing

Stuff handle, and seam cast-on edge together using mattress stitch. (The angle of the seam should match that of the seam at the top of the piece.)

Center bound-off edges of bristles on the wide end of the handle, and attach bristles to the handle using mattress stitch. Before finishing the seam, stuff bristles and attach 18mm eyes to the third ridge down from the top of the piece.

Weave in loose ends.

Tube Front

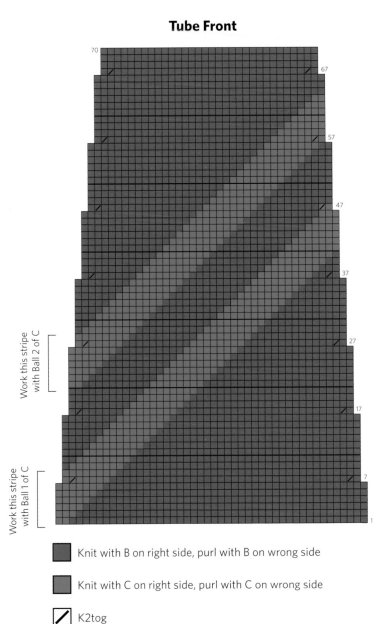

70

67

57

47

37

27

17

7

1

Work this stripe with Ball 2 of C

Work this stripe with Ball 1 of C

Tube Back

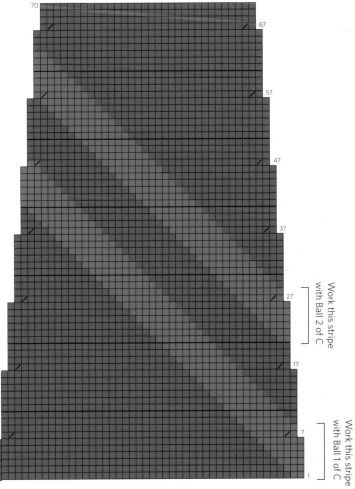

70

67

57

47

37

27

17

7

1

Work this stripe with Ball 2 of C

Work this stripe with Ball 1 of C

![B]	Knit with B on right side, purl with B on wrong side
![C]	Knit with C on right side, purl with C on wrong side
![K2tog]	K2tog

- When switching colors, twist the old color once around the new color on the backside of the piece before working the first stitch in the new color. (See Intarsia Color Change on page 150.)
- When working a section of C stitches between two sections of B stitches, wrap B once around C in the middle of the C section on the purl side to maintain even tension.
- After working the Tube Front chart, break the yarn, and place the stitches onto a spare circular needle or waste yarn to work later.

Big Mike

Who're you calling a meathead? This hefty hamburger will have you know he's part of a low-cal, high-fiber diet. Billions of customers agree that he's an unusual combination of rare and well done.

Note: Big Mike's toppings come à la carte, so you can have him your way. Or invent some toppings of your own!

BOTTOM BUN (worked top to bottom)

Increase Section

With A, cast on 4 stitches onto one DPN.
Rnd 1 (work as I-cord): [Kfb] 4 times (8 sts).

Distribute stitches onto 3 needles to continue to work in a round.
Rnd 2: [Kfb] 8 times (16 sts).
Rnd 3: Knit.
Rnd 4: [Kfb, k1] 8 times (24 sts).
Rnd 5: Knit.
Rnd 6: [Kfb, k2] 8 times (32 sts).
Rnd 7: Knit.
Rnds 8–35: Continue to increase 8 stitches every other round, with the number of knit stitches after Kfb increasing by one each time, until there are 144 stitches on the needle. Along the way, you should switch to using the circular needle whenever it's more comfortable.
Rnds 36–41: Knit (6 rnds).

Decrease Section

Rnd 1: [K2tog, k16] 8 times (136 sts).
Rnd 2: Knit.
Rnds 3–30: Continue to decrease 8 stitches every other round, with the number of knit stitches after K2tog

decreasing by one each time, until there are 24 stitches on the needles. Along the way, switch to using the double-pointed needles whenever it's more comfortable.

Lay piece flat, so that it's in a circular shape, without any wrinkles, and stuff about halfway full, so that it's filled out but is as flat as possible.
Rnd 31: Knit.
Rnd 32: [K2tog, k1] 8 times (16 sts).
Rnd 33: [K2tog] 8 times (8 sts).

Break yarn, leaving a long tail, and draw tightly through the stitches with a tapestry needle.

TOP BUN (worked bottom to top)

With A, work the same as the bottom bun until you reach the decrease section. Work decrease rounds the same as in bottom bun, but knit two rounds between each decrease round instead of one round. Continue until 96 stitches are on the needle.

Next, decrease 8 stitches every other round until 24 stitches are on the needle(s).

Lay piece flat and stuff—the stuffed piece should be thicker than the bottom bun.

Attach eyes, placed between the second and third decrease rounds, and spaced two decreases apart.

Finish the same way as the bottom bun, starting with Round 31 in the decrease section.

Size
14" (35.5cm) wide and 10" (25.5cm) tall

Skill Level
Intermediate

Techniques
Stranded color knitting (page 151)

Yarn
Bulky yarn in 6 colors plus small amount of white

Sample knit with Cascade 128 Superwash, 100% wool, 3½ oz (100g), 128 yds (117m)
3 skeins (384 yds/351m) of 1961 Camel (A)
2 skeins (256 yds/234m) of 1962 Brown Bear (B)
Less than 1 skein (128 yds/117m) of 821 Daffodil (C)
Less than 1 skein (128 yds/117m) of 802 Green Apple (D)
1 skein (128 yds/117m) of 893 Ruby (E)
Less than 1 skein (128 yds/117m) each of 822 Pumpkin (F) and 817 Ecru (G)

Needles
Set of size 8 US (5.0mm) double-pointed needles
Size 8 US (5.0mm) circular needle (See Needle Options on page 14)

Other Supplies
One pair of size 25mm safety eyes
Stuffing

Gauge
2" (5cm) = 8 stitches and 12 rows in stockinette stitch (knit on RS, purl on WS)

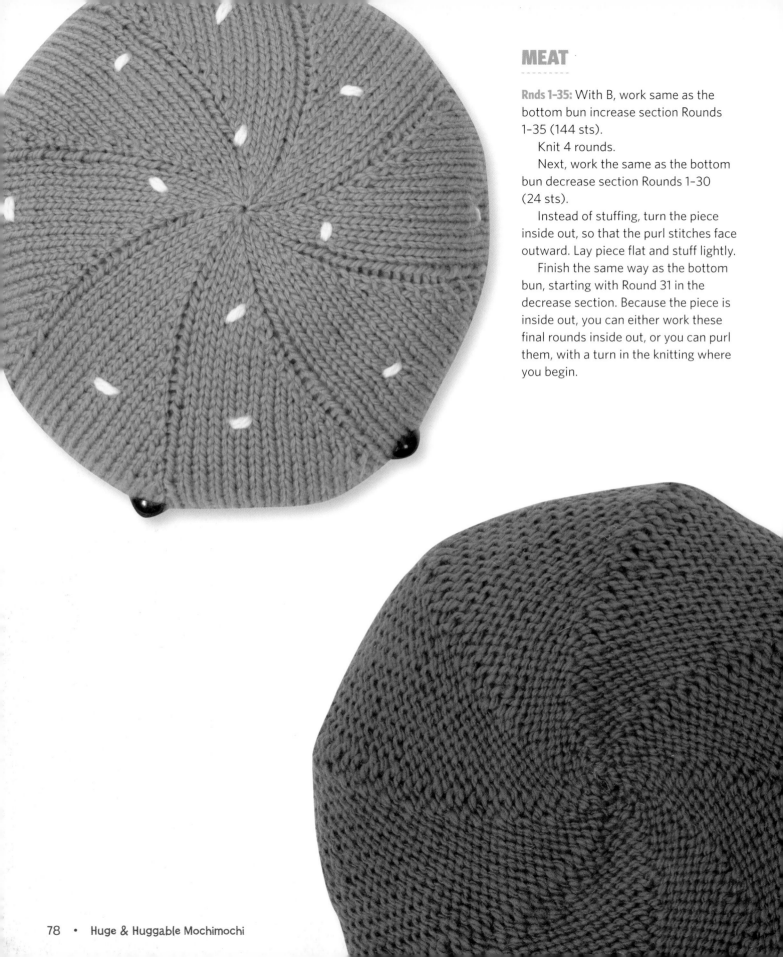

MEAT

Rnds 1–35: With B, work same as the bottom bun increase section Rounds 1–35 (144 sts).

Knit 4 rounds.

Next, work the same as the bottom bun decrease section Rounds 1–30 (24 sts).

Instead of stuffing, turn the piece inside out, so that the purl stitches face outward. Lay piece flat and stuff lightly.

Finish the same way as the bottom bun, starting with Round 31 in the decrease section. Because the piece is inside out, you can either work these final rounds inside out, or you can purl them, with a turn in the knitting where you begin.

Row 6: [Kfb] twice, p2, [kfb] twice (10 sts).
Rows 7–9: Work as established.
Row 10: [Kfb] 4 times, p2, [kfb] 4 times (18 sts).
Rows 11–13: Work as established.
Row 14: [Kfb] 8 times, p2, [kfb] 8 times (34 sts).
Rows 15–17: Work as established.
Row 18: [K2tog] 8 times, p2, [k2tog] 8 times (18 sts).
Rows 19–21: Work as established.
Row 22: [Kfb] 8 times, p2, [kfb] 8 times (34 sts).
Rows 23–27: Work as established.
Row 28: [K2tog] 8 times, p2, [k2tog] 8 times (18 sts).
Rows 29–31: Work as established.
Row 32: [Kfb] 8 times, p2, [kfb] 8 times (34 sts).
Row 33: Work as established.
Row 34: [Kfb] 16 times, p2, [kfb] 16 times (66 sts).
Rows 35–37: Work as established.
Row 38: [K2tog] 16 times, p2, [k2tog] 16 times (34 sts).

CHEESE

With C, cast on 40 stitches onto the circular needle to work flat.

Beginning with a purl row, work 50 rows of stockinette stitch.

Bind off all stitches.

LETTUCE

With D, cast on 4 stitches onto the circular needle to work flat.
Row 1: P1, k2, p1.
Row 2: K1, p2, k1.
Row 3: P1, k2, p1.
Row 4: Kfb, p2, kfb (6 sts).
Row 5: Work as established, knitting the purl stitches from the previous row and purling the knit stitches from the previous row.

Rows 39–41: Work as established.
Row 42: [Kfb] 16 times, p2, [kfb] 16 times (66 sts).
Rows 43–47: Work as established.
Row 48: [K2tog] 16 times, p2, [k2tog] 16 times (34 sts).
Rows 49–51: Work as established.
Row 52: [Kfb] 16 times, p2, [kfb] 16 times (66 sts).
Rows 53–57: Work as established.
Row 58: [K2tog] 16 times, p2, [k2tog] 16 times (34 sts).
Rows 59–61: Work as established.
Row 62: [Kfb] 16 times, p2, [kfb] 16 times (66 sts).
Rows 63–67: Work as established.
Row 68: [K2tog] 16 times, p2, [k2tog] 16 times (34 sts).
Row 69: Work as established.
Row 70: [K2tog] 8 times, p2, [k2tog] 8 times (18 sts).

Row 71: Work as established.
Row 72: [Kfb] 8 times, p2, [kfb] 8 times (34 sts).
Rows 73–77: Work as established.
Row 78: [K2tog] 8 times, p2, [k2tog] 8 times (18 sts).
Row 79: Work as established.
Row 80: [K2tog] 4 times, p2, [k2tog] 4 times (10 sts).
Row 81: Work as established.
Row 82: [K2tog] twice, p2, [k2tog] twice (6 sts).
Row 83: Work as established.
Bind off all stitches.

TOMATO

With E, cast on 4 stitches onto one DPN.
Rnd 1 (work as I-cord): [Kfb] 4 times (8 sts).

Distribute stitches onto 3 needles to continue to work in a round.
Rnd 2: [Kfb] 8 times (16 sts).
Rnd 3 and all odd-numbered rnds through Rnd 13: Knit.
Rnd 4: [Kfb, k1] 8 times (24 sts).
Rnd 6: [Kfb, k2] 8 times (32 sts).
Rnd 8: [Kfb, k3] 8 times (40 sts).
Rnd 10: [Kfb, k4] 8 times (48 sts).
Rnd 12: [Kfb, k5] 8 times (56 sts).
Switch to using the circular needle now or whenever it's comfortable.
Rnd 14: [Kfb, k6] 8 times (64 sts).
Beginning with the next round, you will incorporate F with E.
Rnd 15: K2E, k4F, [k4E, k4F] to last 2 stitches, k2E.
In the following even-numbered rounds 16–28, work as established, working the previous round's E stitches in E and the F stitches in F.
Rnd 16: [Kfb, k7] 8 times (72 sts).
Rnd 17: K2E, k5F, [k4E, k5F] to last 2 stitches, k2E.
Rnd 18: [Kfb, k8] 8 times (80 sts).
Rnd 19: K2E, k6F, [k4E, k6F] to last 2 stitches, k2E.
Rnd 20: [Kfb, k9] 8 times (88 sts).
Rnd 21: K2E, k7F, [k4E, k7F] to last 2 stitches, k2E.
Rnd 22: [Kfb, k10] 8 times (96 sts).
Rnd 23: K2E, k8F, [k4E, k8F] to last 2 stitches, k2E.
Rnd 24: [Kfb, k11] 8 times (104 sts).
Rnd 25: K2E, k9F, [k4E, k9F] to last 2 stitches, k2E.

Rnd 26: [Kfb, k12] 8 times (112 sts).
Rnd 27: K2E, k10F, [k4E, k10F] to last 2 stitches, k2E.
Rnd 28: [Kfb, k13] 8 times (120 sts).

Break F, and continue to work with E only.
Rnd 29: Knit.
Rnd 30: [Kfb, k14] 8 times (128 sts).
Rnd 31: Knit.
Rnd 32: [Kfb, k15] 8 times (136 sts).
Rnd 33: Knit.
Rnd 34: [Kfb, k16] 8 times (144 sts).
Rnds 35 and 36: Knit.
Rnd 37: [K2tog, k16] 8 times (136 sts).
Rnd 38: Knit.
Rnd 39: [K2tog, k15] 8 times (128 sts).
Rnd 40: Knit.
Rnd 41: [K2tog, k14] 8 times (120 sts).
Rnd 42: Knit.
Rnd 43: [K2tog, k13] 8 times (112 sts).

Beginning with the next round, you will again incorporate F with E. When working the odd-numbered rounds 45–57, work as established, working the previous round's E stitches in E and the F stitches in F.
Rnd 44: K2E, k10F, [k4E, k10F] to last 2 stitches, k2E.
Rnd 45: [K2tog, k12] 8 times (104 sts).
Rnd 46: K2E, k9F, [k4E, k9F] to last 2 stitches, k2E.
Rnd 47: [K2tog, k11] 8 times (96 sts).
Rnd 48: K2E, k8F, [k4E, k8F] to last 2 stitches, k2E.
Rnd 49: [K2tog, k10] 8 times (88 sts).
Rnd 50: K2E, k7F, [k4E, k7F] to last 2 stitches, k2E.

Rnd 51: [K2tog, k9] 8 times (80 sts).
Rnd 52: K2E, k6F, [k4E, k6F] to last 2 stitches, k2E.
Rnd 53: [K2tog, k8] 8 times (72 sts).
Rnd 54: K2E, k5F, [k4E, k5F] to last 2 stitches, k2E.
Rnd 55: [K2tog, k7] 8 times (64 sts).
Rnd 56: K2E, k4F, [k4E, k4F] to last 2 stitches, k2E.
Rnd 57: [K2tog, k6] 8 times (56 sts).

Break F, and continue to work with E only.

Switch to using the DPNs now or whenever it's comfortable.
Rnd 58: [K2tog, k5] 8 times (48 sts).
Rnd 59: Knit.
Rnd 60: [K2tog, k4] 8 times (40 sts).
Rnd 61: Knit.
Rnd 62: [K2tog, k3] 8 times (32 sts).
Rnd 63: Knit.
Rnd 64: [K2tog, k2] 8 times (24 sts).
Rnd 65: Knit.
Rnd 66: [K2tog, k1] 8 times (16 sts).
Rnd 67: [K2tog] 8 times (8 sts).

Yes, I would like fries with me.

Arthur

The biggest pencil you'll ever behold, Arthur may not cure writer's block, but you can lean on him when the spelling gets tough. He'll be working on his autobiography when you don't need him.

> I was born into a literary family. Dad was a crayon and Mom was a piece of chalk.

PENCIL

With A, cast on 4 stitches onto one DPN.
Rnd 1 (work as I-cord): [Kfb] 4 times (8 sts).
　Distribute stitches onto 3 needles to continue to work in a round.
Rnd 2: [Kfb] 8 times (16 sts).
Rnd 3: Knit.
Rnd 4: [Kfb, k1] 8 times (24 sts).
Rnd 5: Knit.
Rnd 6: [Kfb, k2] 8 times (32 sts).
Rnd 7: Knit.
Rnd 8: [Kfb, k3] 8 times (40 sts).
Rnds 9–18: Knit (10 rnds).
　Switch to B.
Rnds 19–21: Knit (3 rnds).
Rnd 22: Purl.
Rnds 23–25: Knit (3 rnds).
Rnd 26: Purl.
Rnds 27 and 28: Knit.
　Switch to C.
Rnds 29–58: Knit (30 rnds).
　You will incorporate D with C in the next 2 rounds.

Size
18" (45.5cm) long

Skill Level
Advanced Beginner

Techniques
Stranded color knitting
(page 151)

Yarn
Super bulky yarn in 5 colors

Sample made with:
Lion Brand Wool-Ease Thick & Quick, 80% acrylic, 20% wool, 6 oz (170g), 106 yds (97m)
Less than 1 skein (106 yds/97m) of 640-103 Blossom (A)
Lion Brand Hometown USA, 100% acrylic, 5 oz (140g), 81 yds (74m)
1 skein (106 yds/97m) or less each of:
135-149 Dallas Grey (B)
135-158 Pittsburgh Yellow (C)
135-214 Virginia Beach (D)
135-153 Oakland Black (E)

Needles
Set of size 10.5 US (6.5mm) double-pointed needles and/ or size 10.5 US (6.5mm) circular needle (See Needle Options on page 14)

Other Supplies
One pair of size 18mm safety eyes
Stuffing

Gauge
2" (5cm) = 5 stitches and 7 rows in stockinette stitch (knit on RS, purl on WS)

Rnd 59: [K1D, k3C] to end.

Rnd 60: K2D, [k1C, k3D] to last 2 stitches, k1C, k1D.

Switch to D only.

Rnds 61 and 62: Knit.

Rnd 63: [K2tog, k3] 8 times (32 sts).

Rnds 64 and 65: Knit.

Stuff piece and attach eyes, placed 5 stitches down from B section, and spaced 6 stitches apart.

Rnd 66: [K2tog, k2] 8 times (24 sts).

Rnds 67 and 68: Knit.

Switch to E.

Rnd 69: [K2tog, k1] 8 times (16 sts).

Rnds 70 and 71: Knit.

Rnd 72: [K2tog, k2] 4 times (12 sts).

Rnds 73 and 74: Knit.

Add a bit more stuffing to the end if necessary.

Rnd 75: [K2tog] 6 times (6 sts).

Break yarn and draw tightly through the stitches with a tapestry needle.

Weave in loose ends.

Roland

Roland the roly-poly is done with a life of hiding under rocks and is ready to let it all hang out in retirement. If only Social Security covered pill bugs.

BODY

Back End

With B, cast on 4 stitches onto one DPN.

Rnd 1 (work as I-cord): [Kfb] 4 times (8 sts).

Distribute stitches onto 3 needles to continue working in a round.

Rnd 2: [Kfb] 8 times (16 sts).

Rnd 3: Knit.

Rnd 4: [Kfb, k1] 8 times (24 sts).

Rnd 5: Knit.

Rnd 6: [Kfb, k2] 8 times (32 sts).

Rnd 7: Knit.

Rnd 8: [Kfb, k3] 8 times (40 sts).

Rnd 9: Knit.

Rnd 10: [Kfb, k4] 8 times (48 sts).

Rnds 11 and 12: Knit.

Rnd 13: [Kfb, k5] 8 times (56 sts).

Rnds 14 and 15: Knit.

Rnd 16: K18. Bind off to end. (Bind off the last stitch by slipping it over the first stitch in the round.)

Place the remaining 18 stitches onto one needle to work the piece flat.

Underside

Rows 1–4: Knit.

Row 5: K3, k2tog, yo, k to last 5 stitches, yo, k2tog, k3.

Rows 6–10: Knit (5 rows).

Row 11: K3, k2tog, yo, k to last 5 stitches, yo, k2tog, k3.

Rows 12–16: Knit (5 rows).

Row 17: K3, k2tog, yo, k to last 5 stitches, yo, k2tog, k3.

Rows 18–22: Knit (5 rows).

Row 23: K3, k2tog, yo, k to last 5 stitches, yo, k2tog, k3.

Rows 24–30: Knit (7 rows).

Row 31: K3, k2tog, yo, k to last 5 stitches, yo, k2tog, k3.

Rows 32–36: Knit (5 rows).

Row 37: K3, k2tog, yo, k to last 5 stitches, yo, k2tog, k3.

Rows 38–42: Knit (5 rows).

Row 43: K3, k2tog, yo, k to last 5 stitches, yo, k2tog, k3.

Rows 44–48: Knit (5 rows).

Row 49: K3, k2tog, yo, k to last 5 stitches, yo, k2tog, k3.

Rows 50–53: Knit (4 rows).

Front End

Instead of turning for the next row, cast on 38 stitches using the backward loop method, and distribute the 56 stitches onto 3 DPNs.

Join in a round, making sure not to twist the stitches.

Rnds 1–3: Knit.

Rnd 4: K31, k2tog, yo, k8, yo, k2tog, k to end.

Rnd 5: Knit.

Rnd 6: [K2tog, k5] 8 times (48 sts).

Rnds 7 and 8: Knit.

Rnd 9: [K2tog, k4] 8 times (40 sts).

Rnds 10 and 11: Knit.

Rnd 12: [K2tog, k3] 8 times (32 sts).

Rnds 13 and 14: Knit.

Rnd 15: [K2tog, k2] 8 times (24 sts).

Rnd 16: Knit.

Rnd 17: [K2tog, k1] 8 times (16 sts).

Rnd 18: Knit.

Rnd 19: [K2tog] 8 times (8 sts).

Break yarn and draw tightly through the stitches with a tapestry needle.

Size
24" (61cm) long

Skill Level
Intermediate

Techniques
Backward loop cast-on (page 148), mattress stitch (page 28), I-cord (page 148)

Yarn
Super bulky yarn in 2 colors

Lion Brand Hometown USA, 100% acrylic, 5 oz (142g), 81 yds (74m)
3 skeins (243 yds/222m) of 135-149 Dallas Grey (A)
2 skeins (162 yds/148m) of 135-105 Detroit Blue (B)

Needles
Set of size 10.5 US (6.5mm) double-pointed needles
Size 10.5 US (6.5mm) circular needle
(See Needle Options on page 14)

Other Supplies
Straight pins
One pair of size 25mm safety eyes
Stuffing

Gauge
2" (5cm) = 5 stitches and 7 rows in stockinette stitch (knit on RS, purl on WS)

SHELL

With A, cast on 37 stitches onto the circular needle to work flat.

Row 1: Sl1, p to last stitch, sl1.

Row 2: K4, [p1, k3] 8 times, k1.

Rows 3–7: Work in established rib for 5 rows, slipping the first and last stitches on the odd-numbered rows.

Row 8: K4, kfb, [p1, k3, kfb] 8 times, k1 (46 sts).

Rows 9–13: Work as established for 5 rows.

Row 14: K5, kfb, [p1, k4, kfb] 8 times, k1 (55 sts).

Rows 15–19: Work as established for 5 rows.

Row 20: K6, kfb, [p1, k5, kfb] 8 times, k1 (64 sts).

Rows 21–25: Work as established for 5 rows.

Row 26: K7, kfb, [p1, k6, kfb] 8 times, k1 (73 sts).

Rows 27–31: Work as established for 5 rows.

Row 32: K8, kfb, [p1, k7, kfb] 8 times, k1 (82 sts).

Rows 33–43: Work as established for 11 rows.

Row 44: K7, k2tog, [p1, k6, k2tog] 8 times, k1 (73 sts).

Rows 45–49: Work as established for 5 rows.

Row 50: K6, k2tog, [p1, k5, k2tog] 8 times, k1 (64 sts).

Rows 51–55: Work as established for 5 rows.

Row 56: K5, k2tog, [p1, k4, k2tog] 8 times, k1 (55 sts).

Rows 57–61: Work as established for 5 rows.

Row 62: K4, k2tog, [p1, k3, k2tog] 8 times, k1 (46 sts).

Rows 63–67: Work as established for 5 rows.

Row 68: K3, k2tog, [p1, k2, k2tog] 8 times, k1 (37 sts).

Rows 69–74: Work as established for 6 rows.

Row 75: Sl1, p to last stitch, sl1. Bind off all stitches.

ANTENNAE

With A, cast on 4 stitches onto one DPN.

Knit a 30-row I-cord.

Break yarn and draw tightly through the stitches with a tapestry needle.

LEGS (make 8)

With B, cast on 4 stitches onto one DPN.

Knit a 30-row I-cord

Break yarn and draw tightly through the stitches with a tapestry needle.

FINISHING

Turn the shell purl side out, and fold the piece lengthwise in half, with the cast-on and bound-off edges meeting. Find the end with the increase and decrease stitches running along the edge, and fit the back end of the body into the curve of this edge. Pin the piece in place with straight pins, aligning the body piece so that the underside area fits between the cast-on and bind-off edges of the shell.

Beginning at one corner of the back end, attach the back end to the shell using mattress stitch, then continue stitching one side of the underside to the shell, following diagram (opposite).

Take a break from attaching the pieces to insert the antennae piece through the two yarn-over holes that you made on the front end of the body, with an equal amount of I-cord sticking out from each hole. Attach the eyes to either side of the antennae, placed 4 stitches down from them.

The antennae and eyes will serve as a place marker as you continue assembling; the space between the two should align with the middle of the shell's edge.

Resume attaching the front end of the body to the shell using mattress stitch, and then continue on to the remaining underside edge. Before finishing the last seam, stuff the piece, making sure to fill out the shell and the front and back ends of the body completely, without stuffing so much that the piece is inflexible.

Once you finish the seam, insert the 8 leg pieces side by side through the yarn-over holes, again with an equal amount of I-cord sticking out from each hole.

Weave in the loose ends on the I-cords by weaving them back through the I-cord, and then making a few stitches through the body to secure.

Weave in loose ends.

Shell/Body Assembly

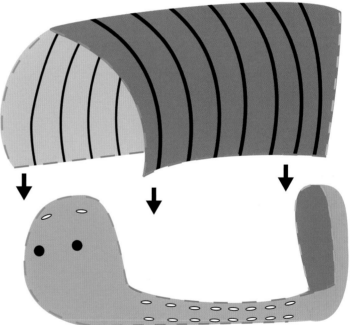

Seam edges of the same colors of dotted lines together in this order:

— — — — Side edge of shell to back end of body

— — — — Cast-on or bound-off edge of shell to one side of body

— — — — Side edge of shell to front end of body

— — — — Cast-on or bound-off edge of shell to remaining side of body

Sometimes the most intimidating guys in the world are actually big softies. To know them is to hug them!

Gentle

Giants

USS *Bubbles*

Sure, she's seaworthy, but it's so much nicer to explore the depths of the bathtub. She'll stay put until the Pacific Ocean is available in lavender scent.

Notes

- This toy is not meant to get wet.
- If you will use stuffing instead of a pillow, sew the side edges of the propellers together after tying them shut.

BODY (worked front to back)

With A, cast on 4 stitches onto one DPN.

Rnd 1 (work as I-cord): [Kfb] 4 times (8 sts).

Distribute stitches onto 3 needles to continue working in a round.

Rnd 2: [Kfb] 8 times (16 sts).

Rnd 3: Knit.

Rnd 4: [Kfb, k1] 8 times (24 sts).

Rnd 5: Knit.

Continue to increase 8 stitches every other round, with the number of knit stitches after kfb increasing by one each time, until there are 96 stitches on the needle. Along the way, you should switch to using the circular needle whenever it's more comfortable.

Knit 24 rounds.

Switch to B.

Knit 1 round, then purl 3 rounds.

Switch to C, and knit 70 rounds.

Switch to B, and knit 1 round.

Next, work in [k1, p1] rib for 4 rounds.

PROPELLERS

Place the first 24 stitches of the round onto one DPN to work flat, separately from the rest of the stitches. You will turn after every row in this section.

Row 1: K1, [kfb] twice, k to last 3 stitches, [kfb] twice, k1 (28 sts).

Row 2: Knit.

Row 3: K1, kfb, k to last 2 stitches, kfb, k1 (30 sts).

Rows 4–18: Knit (15 rows).

Row 19: K1, k2tog, k to last 3 stitches, k2tog, k1 (28 sts).

Row 20: Knit.

Row 21: K1, [k2tog] twice, k to last 5 stitches, [k2tog] twice, k1 (24 sts).

Row 22: Knit.

Row 23: Work same as Row 21 (20 sts).

Row 24: Knit.

Row 25: Work same as Row 21 (16 sts).

Row 26: Knit.

Row 27: K1, [k2tog] 3 times, k2, [k2tog] 3 times, k1 (10 sts).

Rows 28–32: Knit (5 rows).

Row 33: K1, [kfb] twice, knit to last 3 stitches, [kfb] twice, k1 (14 sts).

Row 34: Knit.

Row 35: Work same as Row 33 (18 sts).

Row 36: Knit.

Row 37: Work same as Row 33 (22 sts).

Row 38: Knit.

Size
Fits a 9" by 20" (23cm x 51cm) cylindrical pillow

Skill Level
Intermediate

Techniques
I-cord (page 148), picking up stitches on a flat piece (page 149), mattress stitch (page 28)

Yarn
Bulky yarn in 4 colors

Sample knit with Knit Picks Brava Bulky, 100% acrylic, 3½ oz (100g), 136 yds (124m) 2 skeins (272 yds/248m) each of:
Cornflower (A)
Dove Heather (B)
Peapod (C)
1 skein (136 yds/124m) of Canary (D)

Needles
Set of size 8 US (5.0mm) double-pointed needles
Size 8 US (5.0mm) circular needle
(See Needle Options on page 14)

Other Supplies
9" by 20" (23cm x 51cm) cylindrical pillow or stuffing
Stuffing (small amount for windows and tower)
2 buttons, approximately 1½" (38mm) in diameter
Thread and needle for attaching buttons
Straight pins

Gauge
2" (5cm) = 7½ stitches and 10 rows in stockinette stitch (knit on RS, purl on WS)

Row 39: K1, kfb, k to last 2 stitches, kfb, k1 (24 sts).
Row 40: Knit.
Row 41: Work same as Row 39 (26 sts).
Rows 42–52: Knit (11 rows).
Row 53: K1, k2tog, k to last 3 stitches, k2tog, k1 (24 sts).
Row 54: Knit.
Row 55: Work same as Row 53 (22 sts).
Row 56: Knit.
Row 57: Work same as Row 53 (20 sts).
Row 58: Knit.
Row 59: K1, [k2tog] twice, k to last 5 stitches, [k2tog] twice, k1 (16 sts).
Row 60: Knit.
Row 61: Work same as Row 59 (12 sts).
Row 62: Knit.
Row 63: Work same as Row 59 (8 sts).
Row 64: Knit.
Row 65: [K2tog] 4 times (4 sts).
Without turning, break yarn and draw tightly through the stitches from right to left with a tapestry needle.

For each of the remaining 3 propellers, place the next 24 stitches from the circular needle onto one DPN, reattach the yarn to the first stitch, and work separately according to the above section.

WINDOWS (make 3)

With D, cast on 48 stitches onto 3 DPNs and join to work in a round.
Rnd 1: Knit.
Rnd 2: [K2tog, k4] 8 times (40 sts).
Rnd 3: Knit.
Rnd 4: [K2tog, k3] 8 times (32 sts).
Rnd 5: Knit.
Rnd 6: [K2tog, k2] 8 times (24 sts).
Rnd 7: Knit.
Rnd 8: [K2tog, k1] 8 times (16 sts).
Rnd 9: Knit.
Rnd 10: [K2tog] 8 times (8 sts).
Break yarn and draw tightly through the stitches with a tapestry needle.

TOWER

With A, cast on 14 stitches onto the circular needle to work flat.
Row 1: Purl.
Row 2: K1, kfb, k to last 2 stitches, kfb, k1 (16 sts).
Row 3: Purl.
Row 4: K1, kfb, k to last 2 stitches, kfb, k1 (18 sts).
Rows 5–25: Work 21 rows of stockinette stitch.
Row 26: K1, k2tog, k to last 3 stitches, k2tog, k1 (16 sts).
Row 27: Purl.
Row 28: K1, k2tog, k to last 3 stitches, k2tog, k1 (14 sts).
Row 29: Purl.
Row 30: Knit.

Work Sides

Instead of turning for the next row, rotate the piece 90 degrees clockwise, and pick up and knit 22 stitches along the adjacent side. Rotate the piece again, and pick up and knit 12 stitches on the cast-on edge, then pick up and knit 22 more stitches along the remaining side (70 sts). Place a marker and join the stitches in a round. (See Picking Up Stitches around the Perimeter of a Piece, page 31.)
Knit 10 rounds.
Bind off all stitches.

For my next adventure, I'll explore the refrigerator to discover a snack.

PERISCOPE

With B, cast on 24 stitches onto 3 DPNs, leaving a tail for seaming, and join to work in a round.

Rnds 1–3: Knit.

Rnd 4: Purl.

Repeat the above 4 rounds 8 times total, until you have worked 8 purl ridges.

Purl 2 more rounds.

Next rnd: [P2tog, p4] 4 times (20 sts).

Knit 12 rounds.

Next rnd: [K2tog, k3] 4 times (16 sts).

Last rnd: [K2tog] 8 times (8 sts).

Break yarn and draw tightly through the stitches with a tapestry needle.

FINISHING

Weave in loose ends on the body, and insert the pillow. Tie two opposing propellers together, and tie the other two together on top of them.

Place 3 windows onto one side of the body. Leaving them loose in the middle to accommodate stuffing, pin around the sides to keep them in place.

Begin attaching the cast-on edges of the windows to the body using mattress stitch. (Be careful not to stitch through the pillow, or else the cover won't be removable.) Before finishing the seam, lightly stuff the windows to make them 3-dimensional.

For window rims, cast on 4 stitches with B onto one DPN.

Knit an I-cord until it fits around the outside of the window. (In the sample, each rim is 12½" [32cm] long.)

Bind off all stitches.

Stitch the cast-on and bind-off edges of the window rims together to form rings, and attach them to the outsides of the windows using back stitch (A, below, left).

Attach button eyes to the body on the A section, placed above the windows and close to the stripe of B.

Lightly stuff the tower, and place it on top of the body, between the first and second windows. (The sides of the tower should align with the vertical rows of knitting on the body.)

Pin the bound-off edges of the tower to the body, and begin attaching it to the body using mattress stitch. Before finishing the seam, add more stuffing to the tower so that it's fully filled out.

Push the closed-up end of the periscope into the middle of the piece, so that the consecutive purl rounds form an edge (B, below, right). Add stuffing to the bottom open end, and then pin the cast-on edge to the top of the tower. Attach the edge to the tower using mattress stitch.

Once attached, bend the periscope in half, pointing forward. Use mattress stitch to sew it in place on the outside. (You will get the best results if you stitch the third and sixth purl ridges together.)

Weave in loose ends.

A. *Adjust the length of the window rims to fit around the windows after you have attached the windows to the main piece.*

B. *Push the closed end of the periscope inside the piece to give it a hollow effect.*

Dawn

Dawn thinks of herself as the ultimate morning person, but she can never seem to get up before the sun rises. It's a mystery to her!

BODY (worked bottom to top)

Increase Section

With A, cast on 4 stitches onto one DPN.

Rnd 1 (work as I-cord): [Kfb] 4 times (8 sts).

　Distribute stitches onto 3 needles to continue working in a round.

Rnd 2: [Kfb] 8 times (16 sts).

Rnd 3: Knit

Rnd 4: [Kfb, k1] 8 times (24 sts).

Rnd 5: Knit.

Rnd 6: [Kfb, k2] 8 times (32 sts).

Rnd 7: Knit.

Rnd 8: [Kfb, k3] 8 times (40 sts).

Rnd 9: Knit.

Rnd 10: [Kfb, k4] 8 times (48 sts).

Rnd 11: Knit.

Rnd 12: [Kfb, k5] 8 times (56 sts).

Rnd 13: Knit.

　Switch to the circular needle now or when it's more comfortable.

Rnd 14: [Kfb, k6] 8 times (64 sts).

Rnds 15 and 16: Knit.

Rnd 17: [Kfb, k7] 8 times (72 sts).

Rnds 18 and 19: Knit.

Rnd 20: [Kfb, k8] 8 times (80 sts).

Rnds 21 and 22: Knit.

Rnd 23: [Kfb, k9] 8 times (88 sts).

Rnds 24 and 25: Knit.

Rnd 26: [Kfb, k10] 8 times (96 sts).

Rnds 27–30: Knit 4 rounds.

Rnd 31: [Kfb, k11] 8 times (104 sts).

Rnds 32–35: Knit (4 rnds).

Rnd 36: [Kfb, k12] 8 times (112 sts).

Rnds 37–44: Knit (8 rnds).

Decrease Section

Rnd 45: [K2tog, k12] 8 times (104 sts).

Rnds 46–49: Knit (4 rnds).

Rnd 50: [K2tog, k11] 8 times (96 sts).

Rnds 51–54: Knit (4 rnds).

Rnd 55: [K2tog, k10] 8 times (88 sts).

Rnds 56 and 57: Knit.

Rnd 58: [K2tog, k9] 8 times (80 sts).

Rnds 59 and 60: Knit.

Rnd 61: [K2tog, k8] 8 times (72 sts).

Rnds 62 and 63: Knit.

Rnd 64: [K2tog, k7] 8 times (64 sts).

Rnds 65 and 66: Knit.

Rnd 67: [K2tog, k6] 8 times (56 sts).

Rnd 68: Knit.

Rnd 69: [K2tog, k5] 8 times (48 sts).

Rnd 70: Knit.

Rnd 71: [K2tog, k4] 8 times (40 sts).

Rnd 72: Knit.

　Switch to DPNs now or when it's more comfortable.

Rnd 73: [K2tog, k3] 8 times (32 sts).

Rnd 74: Knit.

Rnd 75: [K2tog, k2] 8 times (24 sts).

Rnd 76: Knit.

　Stuff the piece, completely filling out the sphere.

　Attach eyes, placed just above the first decrease round, and spaced 12 stitches apart.

Rnd 77: [K2tog, k1] 8 times (16 sts).

Rnd 78: [K2tog] 8 times (8 sts).

　Break yarn and draw tightly through the stitches with a tapestry needle.

Size
Circumference is 40"
(101.5cm)

Skill Level
Advanced Beginner

Techniques
Picking up stitches on a flat piece (page 149), I-cord (page 148), mattress stitch (page 28)

Yarn
Super bulky yarn in 3 colors

Sample knit with Spud & Chloë Outer, 65% wool, 35% cotton, 3½ oz (100g), 60 yds (55m)
4 skeins (240 yds/219m) of Cornsilk 7208 (A)
1 skein (60 yds/55m) or less each of:
Rocket 7211 (B)
Cedar 7209 (C)

Needles
Set of size 9 US (5.5mm) double-pointed needles
Size 9 US (5.5mm) circular needle
(See Needle Options on page 14)

Other Supplies
One pair of size 25mm safety eyes
Stuffing
Straight pins

Gauge
2" (5cm) = 6 stitches and 8½ rows in stockinette stitch (knit on RS, purl on WS)

RAYS (make 4 with B and 4 with C)

With B or C, cast on 28 stitches onto 3 DPNs, leaving a tail of 18" (45.5cm) for seaming, and join to work in a round.

Rnds 1–3: Knit.
Rnd 4: K2tog, k10, [k2tog] twice, k10, k2tog (24 sts).
Rnds 5 and 6: Knit.
Rnd 7: K2tog, k8, [k2tog] twice, k8, k2tog (20 sts).
Rnds 8 and 9: Knit.
Rnd 10: K2tog, k6, [k2tog] twice, k6, k2tog (16 sts).
Rnds 11 and 12: Knit.
Rnd 13: K2tog, k4, [k2tog] twice, k4, k2tog (12 sts).
Rnds 14 and 15: Knit.
Rnd 16: K2tog, k2, [k2tog] twice, k2, k2tog (8 sts).
Rnds 17 and 18: Knit.

Break yarn and draw tightly through the stitches with a tapestry needle.

ARMS (make 2)

With A, cast on 6 stitches onto 3 DPNs, leaving a tail of 8" (20.5cm) for seaming, and join to work in a round.

First round: [Kfb] 6 times (12 sts).
  Knit 12 rounds.
  Stuff piece.
Last round: [K2tog] 6 times (6 sts).
  Break yarn and draw tightly through the stitches with a tapestry needle.

Thumb

With A, pick up and knit 2 horizontal stitches, placed about 6 stitches up from the closed end of the piece.
  Knit 2 rows of I-cord.
  Break yarn and draw tightly through the stitches with a tapestry needle.

FINISHING

Stuff the rays. Pin 4 rays of the same color to the top, the bottom, and each side of the body. They should be evenly spaced, with the decrease "seams" at the sides. Using the tails you left when casting on, attach the rays to the body using mattress stitch.

Once you have attached the first 4 rays, pin the remaining 4 onto the sphere spaced evenly between the already attached rays. (There may or may not be a gap between each ray, but the important thing is to make the spacing as even as possible.) Attach these 4 rays with mattress stitch.

Position the arms onto the body, 6 stitches in front of the 2 side rays, and use the tails left over from the cast-on to attach them to the body at a downward angle.

Weave in loose ends.

Maybe I'm not the brightest star in the galaxy, but I know how to warm up a room with my shining personality!

Buddy Boy

If he rolls over you, it's just a sign of affection. Just don't introduce him to your blown glass collection.

BODY

Base and Sides

With A, cast on 26 stitches onto the circular needle to work flat.

Beginning with a purl row, work 56 rows of stockinette stitch.

Instead of turning for the next row, rotate the piece 90 degrees clockwise, and pick up and knit 41 stitches along the adjacent side. Rotate the piece again, and pick up and knit 24 stitches on the cast-on edge. Finally, pick up and knit 41 more stitches along the remaining side (132 sts). Place a marker. You will now work these stitches in the round. (See Picking Up Stitches around the Perimeter of a Piece, page 33.)

Knit 6 rounds.

Work the next 9 rounds according to the Flames chart (page 105), incorporating B.

Switch to B only, and knit 4 more rounds.

Hood/Bed

Knit 26, then bind off to the end of the round, using the first stitch in the round to bind off the last stitch.

Knit the remaining 25 stitches.

Turn and, beginning with a purl row, work 55 rows of stockinette stitch.

Bind off all stitches.

CAB

With C, cast on 80 stitches onto the circular needle.

Being careful not to twist the stitches, place a marker and join in a round.

Rnds 1 and 2: Knit.
Rnd 3: K38, k2tog, k24, ssk, k14 (78 sts).
Rnds 4 and 5: Knit.
Rnd 6: K37, k2tog, k24, ssk, k13 (76 sts).
Rnds 7 and 8: Knit.
Rnd 9: K36, k2tog, k24, ssk, k12 (74 sts).
Rnds 10 and 11: Knit.
Rnd 12: K35, k2tog, k24, ssk, k11 (72 sts).
Rnds 13 and 14: Knit.
Rnd 15: K34, k2tog, k24, ssk, k10 (70 sts).
Rnd 16: Knit.
Switch to B.
Rnds 17 and 18: Knit.
Rnd 19: K24, then bind off to the end of the round, using the first stitch in the round to bind off the last stitch.
Row 20: Knit the remaining 23 stitches. Turn to continue working flat.
Rows 21–31: Beginning with a purl row, work 11 rows of stockinette stitch.
Bind off all stitches.

TIRES (make 4)

With E, cast on 4 stitches onto one DPN.
Rnd 1 (work as I-cord): [Kfb] 4 times (8 sts).
Distribute stitches onto 3 needles to continue working in a round.
Rnd 2: [Kfb] 8 times (16 sts).
Switch to C.
Rnd 3: Knit.
Rnd 4: [Kfb, k1] 8 times (24 sts).
Rnd 5: Knit.
Rnd 6: [Kfb, k2] 8 times (32 sts).

Size
20" (51cm) wide by 20" (51cm) tall (including top lights)

Skill Level
Experienced

Techniques
Picking up stitches on a flat piece (page 149), stranded color knitting (page 151), mattress stitch (page 28), duplicate stitch (page 35)

Yarn
Super bulky yarn in 5 colors

Sample made with Lion Brand Hometown USA, 100% acrylic, 5 oz (142g), 81 yds (74m) 2 skeins (162 yds/148m) of 135-133 Syracuse Orange (A) 3 skeins (243 yds/222m) of 135-107 Charlotte Blue (B) 3 skeins (243 yds/222m) of 135-149 Dallas Grey (C) 1 skein (81 yds/74m) of 135-158 Pittsburgh Yellow (D) Wool-Ease Thick & Quick Prints, 80% acrylic, 20% wool, 5 oz (142g), 87 yds (79.5m) 4 skeins (348 yds/318m) of 640-503 Granite (E)

Needles
Size 10.5 US (6.5mm) circular needle Set of size 10.5 US (6.5mm) double-pointed needles (optional) (See Needle Options on page 14)

Other Supplies
One pair of size 25mm safety eyes Stuffing

Gauge
2" (5cm) = 5 stitches and 7 rows in stockinette stitch (knit on RS, purl on WS)

Note: Pfb = purl through the front and the back of the stitch, increasing the stitch count by 1

Rnd 7: Knit.

Rnd 8: [Kfb, k3] 8 times (40 sts).

Switch to the circular needle.

Rnd 9: Knit.

Rnd 10: [Kfb, k4] 8 times (48 sts).

Switch to E.

Rnd 11: Knit.

Rnd 12: [Kfb, k5] 8 times (56 sts).

Rnd 13: Knit.

Rnd 14: [Kfb, k6] 8 times (64 sts).

Rnd 15: Knit.

Rnd 16: [Kfb, k7] 8 times (72 sts).

Rnd 17: Purl.

Rnd 18: [Pfb, p8] 8 times (80 sts).

Rnd 19: Purl.

Rnds 20–31: [K1, p3] to end (for 12 rnds).

Rnd 32: Purl.

Rnd 33: [P2tog, p8] 8 times (72 sts).

Rnd 34: Purl.

Rnd 35: [K2tog, k7] 8 times (64 sts).

Rnd 36: Knit.

Rnd 37: [K2tog, k6] 8 times (56 sts).

Rnd 38: Knit.

Rnd 39: [K2tog, k5] 8 times (48 sts).

Switch to C.

Rnd 40: Knit.

Rnd 41: [K2tog, k4] 8 times (40 sts).

Rnd 42: Knit.

Switch to DPNs.

Rnd 43: [K2tog, k3] 8 times (32 sts).

Rnd 44: Knit.

Rnd 45: [K2tog, k2] 8 times (24 sts).

Stuff piece, filling it out completely without losing its tire shape.

Switch to E.

Rnd 46: Knit.

Rnd 47: [K2tog, k1] 8 times (16 sts).

Break yarn and draw tightly through the stitches with a tapestry needle.

AXLES (make 2)

With C, cast on 18 stitches onto 3 DPNs and join to work in a round.

Knit 12 rounds.

Bind off all stitches.

HEADLIGHTS

With D, cast on 11 stitches onto one DPN to work flat.

Row 1: P1, [k1, p1] to end.

Row 2: K1, [p1, k1] to end.

Rows 3–11: Work in established rib pattern for 9 rows.

Switch to C.

Row 12: Knit.

Row 13: P1C, [p1C, p1E] to end.

Row 14: K1C, [k1E, k1C] to end.

Rows 15–22: Repeat Rows 13 and 14 four times.

Switch to C only.

Row 23: Purl.

Switch to D.

Row 24: Knit.

Row 25: P1, [k1, p1] to end.

Row 26: K1, [p1, k1] to end.

Rows 27–34: Work in established rib pattern for 8 rows.

Bind off all stitches as established.

TOP LIGHTS (make 3)

With C, cast on 4 stitches onto one DPN.

Rnd 1 (work as I-cord): [Kfb] 4 times (8 sts).

Distribute stitches onto 3 needles to continue working in a round.

Rnd 2: [Kfb] 8 times (16 sts).

Rnd 3: Knit.

Rnd 4: [Kfb, k3] 4 times (20 sts).

Rnd 5: Knit.

Switch to D.

Rnds 6 and 7: Knit.

Rnd 8: [K2tog, k3] 4 times (16 sts).

Rnd 9: Knit.

Stuff piece.

Rnd 10: [K2tog] 8 times (8 sts).

Break yarn and draw tightly through the stitches with a tapestry needle.

FINISHING

All of the following seaming and attaching should be done using mattress stitch.

Lay the edges of the hood/bed flap over the bound-off stitches on the body piece, and secure in place with a few straight pins or DPNs.

Beginning in one corner, seam the sides of the flap to the bound-off edge, following the diagram (opposite). Before finishing the seam, stuff the piece, making sure to fill it out completely without overstuffing. The smooth end of the body without the flap seam will become the front of the truck.

Lay the edges of the flap on the cab piece over that piece's bound-off stitches, pin in place, and, beginning in one corner, seam together. The side with the longer seamed edge will become the front of the cab.

Place the cab on top of the body, with the front of the cab aligned just behind the first "flame" on the side of the body. Secure the cab to the body with straight pins or DPNs. Attach the cast-on edges of the cab to the body, making your stitches in straight lines to give the cab a rectangular shape. Before finishing the seam, stuff the cab and attach eyes to the front of the cab, placed halfway down the piece and spaced 10 stitches apart.

With B, embroider 4 vertical window frames onto the cab using 2 columns of duplicate stitch for each. The 2 frames on the front window should follow the decrease stitches on the cab, emphasizing the slope of the piece. The 2 frames on the back of the piece should stand straight up on either side of the back side.

Turn the headlights piece on its side, with the knit stitches in the middle of the piece facing forward, and pin it in place on the front of the body. Attach it to the body around the edges.

Pin the 3 top lights on the top front of the cab, spaced evenly apart. Attach them to the cab, stitching around the areas of the lights that touch the cab.

Stuff an axle, and attach its cast-on edge to the increase side of one tire.

Attach its bound-off edge to another tire's increase side. Repeat with the other axle and pair of tires.

Attach each pair of front and back tires to each other in the areas where they touch.

Place the body on top of the four tires. Note where the body touches the tires, and attach the body to each tire in those areas. For a more secure attachment, attach the body to the tires in two places—stitch one seam along the outer edge of the body, and stitch another farther in on the tire and on the body's underside.

Weave in all loose ends.

Flames

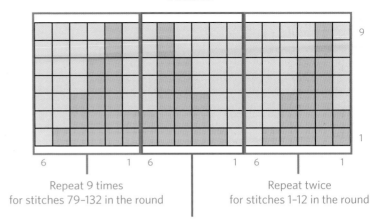

Repeat 9 times
for stitches 79–132 in the round

Repeat 11 times
for stitches 13–78 in the round

Repeat twice
for stitches 1–12 in the round

◻ Knit with A   ◻ Knit with B

Truck Assembly

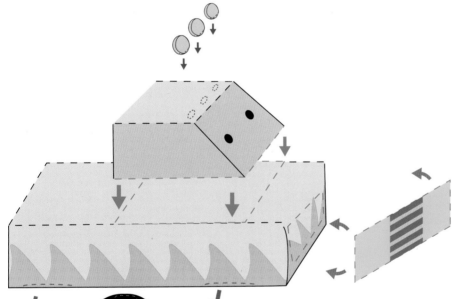

Seam edges of the same colors of dotted lines together in this order:

— — — — — Flaps on body and cab pieces

— — — — Cab to body

— — — — Headlights to body

— — — — Top lights to cab

— — — — Axles to tires

— — — — Front tires to back tires

— — — — Body to tires

Cityzens

They've had enough of the big city and are trying out the simple life for a change. Now they just need to find a place that delivers sushi around here . . .

BUILDING 1 (building with 2 antennae)

With A, cast on 52 stitches onto the circular needle.

Place a beginning-of-round marker. Being careful not to twist the stitches, join in a round.

Rnd 1: K26, pm, k26.

Rnd 2: K1, kfb, k to 2 stitches before marker, kfb, k1, sm, k1, kfb, k to last 2 stitches, kfb, k1 (56 sts).

Rnd 3: Knit.

Rnd 4: Work same as Round 2 (60 sts).

You can remove the halfway marker after Round 4.

Rnds 5–52: Incorporate B and work according to the Window chart (page 110) skipping windows in a random fashion for a lit/unlit effect, until there are 9 rows of windows.

Rnds 53–55: Work Rounds 1–3 of the chart to add one more row of windows.

Switch to A only.

Rnds 56 and 57: Knit.

Rnd 58: K1, k2tog, k24, k2tog, k2, k2tog, k24, k2tog, k1 (56 sts).

Bind off all stitches.

Antennae

With B, cast on 6 stitches onto 3 DPNs, leaving a tail for attaching, and join to work in a round.

Knit 14 rounds, stuffing the piece as you go.

Break yarn and draw tightly through the stitches with a tapestry needle.

Make another piece in the same way as the first, except with 18 rounds of knitting instead of 14.

BUILDING 2 (Empire State Building)

Note: When binding off stitches in the middle of a round, always begin by working 2 stitches, then slip the first stitch over the second.

With A, cast on 62 stitches onto the circular needle.

Place a beginning-of-round marker. Being careful not to twist the stitches, join in a round.

Sizes
Buildings range from 11" (28cm) to 29" (74cm) tall

Skill Level
Intermediate

Techniques
Stranded color knitting (page 151), mattress stitch (page 28)

Yarn
Super bulky yarn in 4 colors

 6

Samples made with Lion Brand Hometown USA, 100% acrylic, 5 oz (140g), 81 yds (74m)
2 skeins (162 yds/148m) of Minneapolis Purple 135-147 (A)
4 skeins (324 yds/296m) of Detroit Blue 135-105 (A)
4 skeins (324 yds/296m) of New Orleans French Berry 135-146 (A)
3 skeins (243 yds/222m) of Pittsburgh Yellow 135-158 (B)

Needles
Size 10.5 US (6.5mm) circular needle
Set of size 10.5 US (6.5mm) double-pointed needles (optional, for spire and antennae) (See Needle Options on page 14)

Other Supplies
5 pairs of size 25mm safety eyes
Stuffing

Gauge
2" (5cm) = 5 stitches and 7 rows in stockinette stitch (knit on RS, purl on WS)

Note: The Window chart (page 110) is used throughout the pattern, with the windows added at the knitter's discretion for a lit/unlit effect.

Rnd 1: K31, pm, k31.

Rnd 2: K1, kfb, k to 2 stitches before marker, kfb, k1, sm, k1, kfb, k to last 2 stitches, kfb, k1 (66 sts).

Rnd 3: Knit.

Rnd 4: Work same as Round 2 (70 sts).

You can remove the halfway marker after Round 4.

Rnds 5–58: Incorporate B and work according to the Window chart (page 110), skipping windows in a random fashion for a lit/unlit effect, until there are 9 rows of windows.

Rnds 59–61: Work Rounds 1–3 of the chart to add one more row of windows.

Switch to A only (without breaking B).

Rnds 62–64: Knit (3 rnds).

Rnd 65: K1, [k1B, k3A] 8 times, k1B, k2A, [k1B, k3A] 8 times, k1B, k1A.

Rnds 66–71: Repeat Round 65 six times.

Switch to A (without breaking B).

Rnd 72: Knit.

Rnd 73: K30, bind off 10 stitches (begin binding off with stitches 31 and 32— see pattern note), k to last 5 stitches, bind off 5 stitches, then continue to bind off 5 stitches at the beginning of the next round (50 sts).

You will now have 2 sections of 25 stitches each, separated by the bound-off stitches.

The stitch that is on the right end of the needle will now become the first stitch in the round.

Rnd 74: Knit to the end of the round.

Rnd 75: K2A, [k1B, k3A] 5 times, k1B, k4A, [k1B, k3A] 5 times, k1B, k2A.

Rnds 76–81: Repeat Round 75 six times.

Switch to A (without breaking B).

Rnd 82: Knit.

Rnd 83: K20, bind off 10, k to last 5 stitches, bind off 5, then bind off 5 stitches at the beginning of the next round (30 sts).

Rnd 84: Knit to the end of the round.

Rnds 85–91: K3A, [k1B, k3A] twice, k1B, k6A, [k1B, k3A] twice, k1B, k3A (7 rnds).

Switch to A (and break B).

Rnd 92: K1, k2tog, k9, k2tog, k2, k2tog, k9, k2tog, k1 (26 sts).

Bind off all stitches.

Spire

With A, cast on 8 stitches onto 3 DPNs, leaving a tail for attaching, and join to work in a round.

Knit 8 rounds, stuffing the piece as you go.

Switch to B, and knit 4 rounds.

Stuff the top of the piece, then break yarn and draw tightly through the stitches with a tapestry needle.

BUILDING 3 (squat building)

With A, cast on 72 stitches onto the circular needle.

Place a beginning-of-round marker. Being careful not to twist the stitches, join in a round.

Rnd 1: K36, pm, k36.

Rnd 2: K1, kfb, k to 2 stitches before marker, kfb, k1, sm, k1, kfb, k to last 2 stitches, kfb, k1 (76 sts).

Rnd 3: Knit.

Rnd 4: Work same as Round 2 (80 sts).

You can remove the halfway marker after Round 4.

Rnds 5–52: Incorporate B and work according to the Window chart (page 110), skipping windows in a random fashion for a lit/unlit effect, until there are 9 rows of windows.

Rnds 53–55: Work Rounds 1–3 of the chart to add one more row of windows.

Switch to A only.

Rnds 56 and 57: Knit.

Rnd 58: K1, k2tog, k34, k2tog, k2, k2tog, k34, k2tog, k1 (76 sts).

Bind off all stitches.

BUILDING 4 (slanted building)

With A, cast on 52 stitches onto the circular needle.

Place a marker at the beginning of the round. Being careful not to twist the stitches, join in a round.

Rnd 1: K26, pm, k26.

Rnd 2: K1, kfb, k to 2 stitches before marker, kfb, k1, sm, k1, kfb, k to last 2 stitches, kfb, k1 (56 sts).

Rnd 3: Knit.

Rnd 4: Work same as Round 2 (60 sts).

You can remove the halfway marker after Round 4.

Rnds 5–52: Incorporate B and work according to the Window chart (page 110), skipping windows in a random fashion for a lit/unlit effect, until there are 8 rows of windows.

Switch to B (without breaking A).

Rnd 53: K25, [k2tog] twice, k1, pm, k1, [k2tog] twice, k to end (56 sts).

Rnd 54: [K1B, k1A] to end.

Rnd 55: Using B only (without breaking A), knit to 5 stitches before marker, [k2tog] twice, k1, sm, k1, [k2tog] twice, k to end (52 sts).

Rnds 56–73: Repeat Rounds 54 and 55 nine more times, until there are 16 stitches on the needle.

Bind off all stitches.

> **Knit us all, and you can be mayor of your own metropolis!**

BUILDING 5 (baby building)

With A, cast on 36 stitches onto the circular needle, and join to work in a round.

Rnd 1: Knit.

Rnd 2: K1, kfb, k14, kfb, k2, kfb, k14, kfb, k1 (40 sts).

Rnds 3 and 4: Knit.

Rnds 5–34: Incorporate B and work according to the Window chart (below), skipping windows in a random fashion for a lit/unlit effect, until there are 5 rows of windows.

Bind off all stitches.

FINISHING

Lay the building flat, so that the beginnings of the rounds are at the right edge of the piece. Seam the cast-on edge closed using mattress stitch. This will be the bottom of the building.

Attach the eyes, placed as shown in the photos, and stuff the piece fully without overstuffing.

For Buildings 1, 3, 4, and 5, seam the bound-off edge using mattress stitch.

For Building 2, make sure that the bound-off stitches toward the top of the piece line up with a front side and back, again with the beginnings of the rounds forming the right edge, and seam together each section of bound-off stitches.

Attach the cast-on edges of the antennae and the spire onto the tops of Buildings 1 and 2 with mattress stitch. Pull the stitches tightly when you stitch across the top seam so that the seam is even and invisible.

Weave in loose ends.

Window

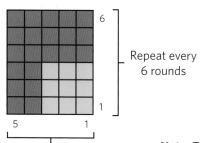

Repeat every 6 rounds

Repeat every 5 stitches in the round

■ Knit with A
□ Knit with B

Note: This chart is written with all windows filled in, or "lit." You can give the effect of unlit windows by replacing sections of B with A in a random fashion. When you skip a window in this way, twist B once around A on the back side of the piece midway through the longer section of A to maintain an even tension.

ALL ABOARD READING

Totem Poles

By
Jennifer Frantz

Illustrated by
Allan Eitzen

STUART WOODS UNNATUR

THE TREE

FIELD GUIDE TO TREES OF NORTH AMERICA

Western Trees

THE COMPLETE WOODSHOP GUIDE

3 STEPS TO A STRONG FAMILY RIC

THE ILLUSTRATED BOOK OF Trees

WOOD WORK

SEEING TREES   Nancy Ross Hugo Robert Llewell

Sobun   BASIC WOODWORKING

TREES OF NORTH AMERICA   Alan

Graham R. Bull   The Complete Woodcarver's Han

Bridgewater & Bridgewater   WOODCARVING BASICS

The WORLD OF TREES   JOHNSO

Taunton's Complete Illustrated Guide to
Woodworking

FIREFLY
ENCYCLOPEDIA
OF TREES

THE MEANING OF
TREES

Tree-o

These vertical friends share a love for multiscoop ice cream cones and studies in woodworking. Their favorite library hangout is the stacks, of course!

BODY

Base

With B, cast on 4 stitches onto one DPN.

Rnd 1 (work as I-cord): [Kfb] 4 times (8 sts).

Distribute stitches onto 3 needles to continue to work in a round.

Rnd 2: [Kfb] 8 times (16 sts).

Rnd 3: Knit.

Rnd 4: [Kfb, k1] 8 times (24 sts).

Switch to C. (Leave B attached, and do the same with C in this section.)

Rnd 5: Knit.

Rnd 6: [Kfb, k2] 8 times (32 sts).

Rnd 7: Knit.

Rnd 8: [Kfb, k3] 8 times (40 sts).

Rnd 9: Knit.

Rnd 10: [Kfb, k4] 8 times (48 sts).

Switch to B.

Rnd 11: Knit.

Rnd 12: [Kfb, k5] 8 times (56 sts).

Rnd 13: Knit.

Rnd 14: [Kfb, k6] 8 times (64 sts).

Rnd 15: Knit.

Rnd 16: [Kfb, k7] 8 times (72 sts).

Switch to C.

Rnd 17: Knit.

Rnd 18: [Kfb, k8] 8 times (80 sts).

Rnd 19: Knit.

Rnd 20: [Kfb, k9] 8 times (88 sts).

Rnd 21: Knit.

Rnd 22: [Kfb, k10] 8 times (96 sts).

Switch to B.

Rnds 23–27: Knit (5 rnds).

3-Row Bobble Stitch

Begin bobble: In the first round, knit into the front and back of the stitch 3 times to make 6 stitches on the right needle.

In the second round, work the stitches as indicated.

Finish bobble: In the third round, work the 6 stitches, then pass the first 5 stitches over the last stitch on the right needle.

Sides

Rnds 1–5: Work as shown in Tree-o 1 chart (page 115).

Switch to A.

Rnds 6–14: Knit (9 rnds).

Rnd 15: [Begin bobble, k7] to end (156 sts).

Rnd 16: [P6, k7] to end.

Rnd 17: [Finish bobble, k7] to end (96 sts).

Rnds 18–26: Knit (9 rnds).

Rnds 27–38: Work 12 rounds as shown in Tree-o 2 chart (page 115).

Rnds 39–59: Switch to A, and work same as Rounds 6–26.

Rnds 60–74: Work 15 rounds as shown in Tree-o 3 chart (page 115).

Rnds 75–95: Switch to A, and work same as Rounds 6–26.

Rnds 96–100: Work 5 rounds as shown in Tree-o 4 chart (page 115).

Rnds 101–106: Switch to C, and knit (6 rnds).

Size

Fits a 9" by 20" (23cm x 51cm) cylindrical pillow

Skill Level

Experienced

Techniques

Stranded color knitting (page 151), 3-row bobble stitch (see box, at left), duplicate stitch (page 35), three-needle bind-off (page 155), mattress stitch (page 28)

Yarn

Bulky yarn in one main color and 3 contrasting colors

Sample knit with Knit Picks Brava Bulky, 100% acrylic, 3½ oz (100g), 136 yds (124m)
3 skeins (408 yds/373m) of Camel Heather (A)
1 skein (136 yds/124m) each of:
Rouge (B)
Canary (C)
Cornflower (D)

Needles

Set of size 8 US (5.0mm) double-pointed needles
Size 8 US (5.0mm) circular needle
(See Needle Options on page 14)

Other Supplies

9" by 20" (23cm x 51cm) cylindrical pillow or stuffing
6 buttons, approximately 1" (2.5cm) in diameter
Thread and needle for attaching buttons
Straight pins

Gauge

2" (5cm) = 7½ stitches and 10 rows in stockinette stitch (knit on RS, purl on WS)

Note: If you will use stuffing instead of a pillow, stitch the top tie to the piece so that it won't come undone.

Top

Switch to A.

Rnd 1: Knit.

Rnds 2–19: [K1, p1] to end (18 rnds).

Rnd 20: [K2tog, yo, k10] 8 times.

Rnds 21–24: Switch to B, and knit (4 rnds).

Rnds 25–28: Switch to D, and knit (4 rnds).

Rnds 29–32: Switch to C, and knit (4 rnds).

Rnds 33–36: Switch to B, and knit (4 rnds).

Rnds 37–40: Switch to D, and knit (4 rnds).

Rnds 41–43: Switch to C, and knit (3 rnds).

Bind off all stitches.

TIE

With D, cast on 3 stitches onto one DPN.

Knit an I-cord until it measures approximately 32" (81cm).

ARMS (make 2)

With A, cast on 12 stitches onto 3 DPNs, leaving a tail for attaching, and join to work in a round.

Rnds 1–10: Knit, stuffing the piece as you go.

Rnd 11: [K2tog] 6 times (6 sts).

Rnd 12: [Kfb] 6 times (12 sts).

Rnds 13–16: Knit (4 rnds).

Stuff the top of the piece.

Rnd 17: [K2tog] 6 times (6 sts).

Break the yarn and draw tightly through the stitches with a tapestry needle.

EARS (make 2)

Work this piece in A unless noted otherwise.

With A, cast on 28 stitches onto 3 DPNs and join to work in a round.

Rnds 1 and 2: Knit.

Rnds 3 and 4: K3A, k8D, k6A, k8D, k3A.

Rnd 5: K1, k2tog, k8D, ssk, k2, k2tog, k8D, ssk, k1 (24 sts).

Rnds 6 and 7: K3A, k6D, k6A, k6D, k3A.

Rnd 8: K1, k2tog, k6D, ssk, k2, k2tog, k6D, ssk, k1 (20 sts).

Switch to A only.

Rnd 9: Knit.

Divide the stitches onto 2 needles, and bind off using the 3-needle bind-off method.

BEAK

With B, cast on 8 stitches onto 3 DPNs, leaving a tail for attaching, and join to work in a round.

Rnds 1–4: Knit.

Rnd 5: [K2tog] 4 times (4 sts).

Rnd 6: Knit.

Break the yarn and draw tightly through the stitches with a tapestry needle.

WINGS (make 2)

With A, cast on 36 stitches onto 3 DPNs and join to work in a round.

Rnds 1 and 2: Knit.

Rnd 3: [K1A, k1B] 4 times, k2A, [k1B, k1A] 4 times, [k1A, k1B] 4 times, k2A, [k1B, k1A] 4 times.

Rnds 4–10: Repeat Round 3 for 7 more rounds.

Switch to A only (and leave B attached).

Rnd 11: Knit.

Rnd 12: K10, BO 16 stitches, k to end (20 sts).

Rnd 13: Knit, pulling the yarn tightly across the WS of the bound-off stitches.

Rnd 14: [K1B, k1A] 5 times, [k1A, k1B] 5 times.

Rnds 15–17: Repeat Round 14 for 3 more rounds.

Switch to A only.

Rnd 18: Knit.

Divide the stitches onto 2 needles, and bind off using the 3-needle bind-off method.

FINISHING

Stuff the pillow inside the body. Weave the tie in and out of the yarn-over holes at the top, gather the ribbed section together, and tie in a bow.

Place the 6 buttons onto the three areas of A, just above the row of bobbles, and spaced 12–14 stitches apart, and pin them in place. Attach the buttons to the body using needle and thread, being careful not to sew them to the pillow underneath.

With C, embroider nostrils onto the bottom face with 4 horizontal stitches that span the width of one knit stitch for each, spaced 2 stitches apart. Embroider the mouth using duplicate stitch as shown in the chart (opposite).

With D, embroider a nose onto the middle face using duplicate stitch as shown in the chart (opposite). Embroider one long vertical stitch directly below the nose, then embroider whiskers with 2 diagonal stitches for each, placed as shown in the photos.

Stuff the beak, and attach its cast-on edge to the middle of the top face, using mattress stitch. Stitch the tip of the beak down onto the body to make it point downward.

Attach the cast-on edges of the arms to either side of the body, just below the row of bobbles, using mattress stitch.

Stuff the ears and wings, and attach their cast-on edges to either side of the body, with their bound-off edges running parallel to the body.

Weave in loose ends.

Tree-o 1

5
1

8   1

Work every
8 stitches in the round

Tree-o 2

38

27

8   1

Work every
8 stitches in the round

Duplicate Stitch Pattern for Bottom Face

Duplicate Stitch Pattern for Middle Face

Tree-o 3

74

70

60

8   1

Work every
8 stitches in the round

Tree-o 4

100

96

8   1

Work every
8 stitches in the round

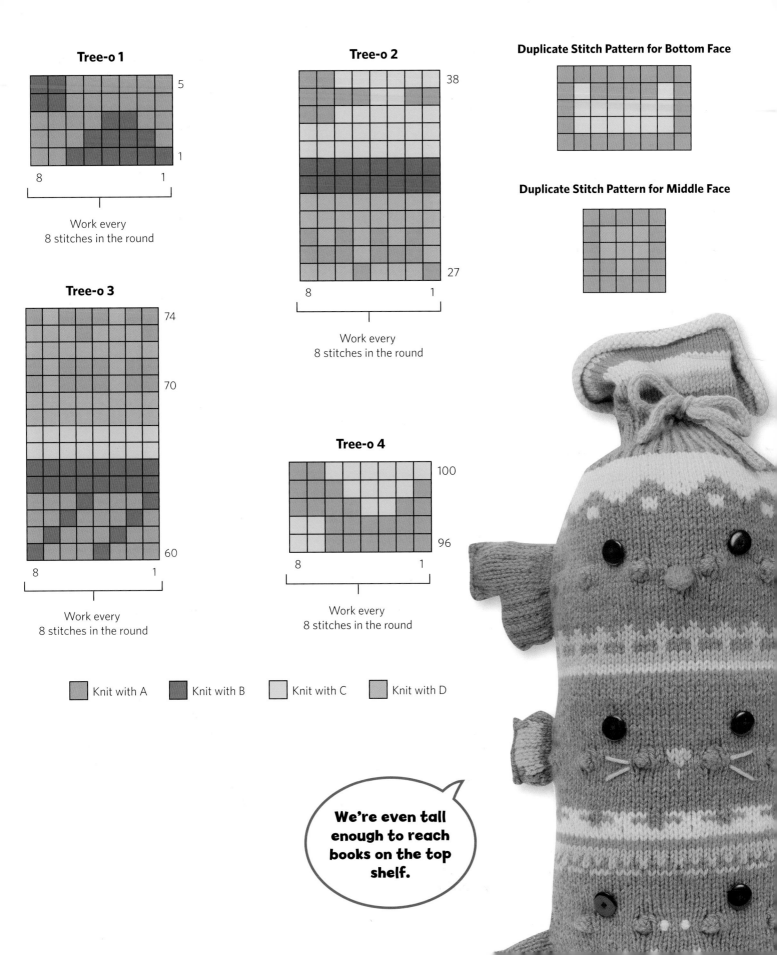

| | Knit with A | | Knit with B | | Knit with C | | Knit with D |

We're even tall
enough to reach
books on the top
shelf.

Practical

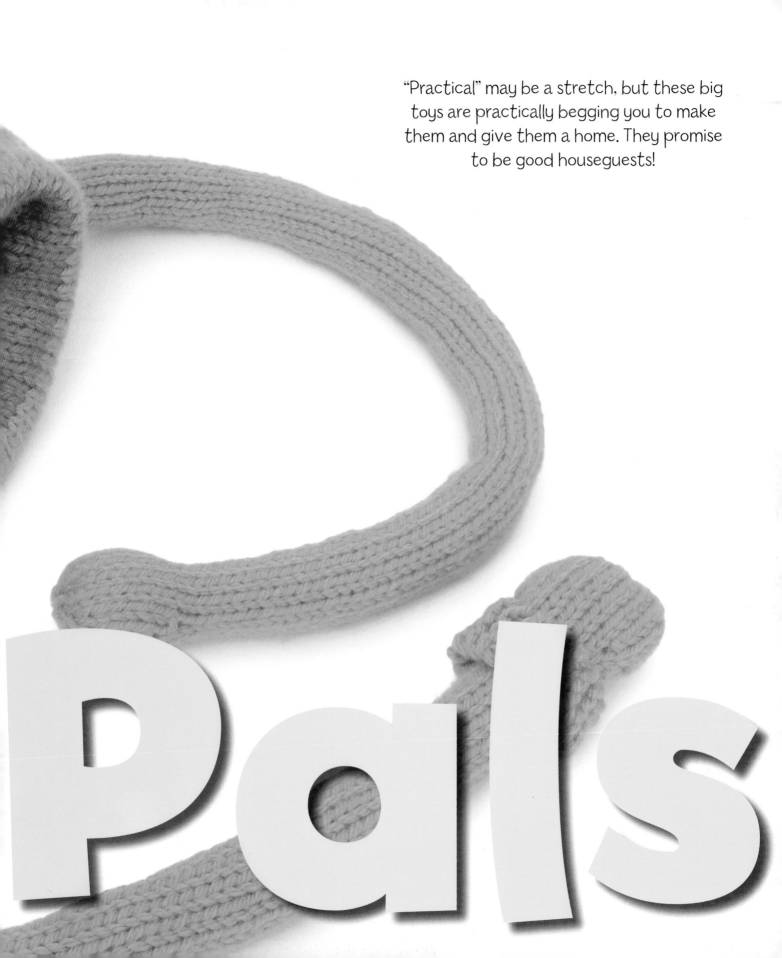

"Practical" may be a stretch, but these big toys are practically begging you to make them and give them a home. They promise to be good houseguests!

Pals

Lupe

A true party animal, Lupe is always ready to celebrate—she'll bring the candy, stashed in her belly! The fun always seems to end badly for her, but popularity comes at a price.

LUPE

Body

Belly

With A, cast on 22 stitches onto the circular needle to work flat.
Row 1: Purl.
Row 2: K1, kfb, k to last 2 stitches, kfb, k1 (24 sts).
Row 3: Purl.
Row 4: K1, kfb, k to last 2 stitches, kfb, k1 (26 sts).
Rows 5–33: Beginning with a purl row, work 29 rows of stockinette stitch.
Row 34: K7, BO 12 (begin binding off with the 8th and 9th stitches), k6 (14 sts).
Row 35: P7, cast on 12 stitches, p7 (26 sts).
Rows 36–64: Beginning with a knit row, work 29 rows of stockinette stitch.
Row 65: P1, p2tog, p to last 3 stitches, p2tog, p1 (24 sts).
Row 66: Knit.
Row 67: P1, p2tog, p to last 3 stitches, p2tog, p1 (22 sts).
Row 68: Knit.

Sides

Instead of turning for the next row, rotate the piece 90 degrees clockwise, and pick up and knit 55 stitches along the adjacent side. Rotate the piece again, and pick up and knit 20 stitches on the cast-on edge. Finally, pick up and knit 55 more stitches along the remaining side (152 sts). Place a marker. You will now work these stitches in the round. (See Picking Up Stitches around the Perimeter of a Piece, page 33.)
Rnds 1–3: Knit.
Rnd 4: [Loop1] to end (page 120). Switch to B.
Rnds 5–9: Knit (5 rnds).
Rnd 10: [Loop1] to end.
Rnds 11–15: Knit (5 rnds).
Rnd 16: [Loop1] to end. Switch to C.
Rnds 17–21: Knit (5 rnds).
Rnd 22: [Loop1] to end.
Rnds 23–27: Knit (5 rnds).
Rnd 28: [Loop1] to end.

Back

Knit 22, then bind off to the end of the round (beginning with stitches 23 and 24). Use the first stitch in the round to bind off the last stitch.

You should now have one stitch on the right end of the needle and 21 stitches on the left. Knit the remaining 21 stitches (22 sts).

Switch to D. You will continue to knit the piece flat.
Row 1: Turn, and purl.
Row 2: K1, kfb, k to last 2 stitches, kfb, k1 (24 sts).
Row 3: Purl.
Row 4: K1, kfb, k to last 2 stitches, kfb, k1 (26 sts).
Row 5: Purl.
Row 6: K1, loop1 to last stitch, k1.
Rows 7–11: Beginning with a purl row, work 5 rows of stockinette stitch.
Row 12: K1, loop1 to last stitch, k1.
Rows 13–24: Repeat Rows 7–12 twice more.
Switch to E.

Size

Lupe is 18" (45.5cm) long (nose to tail) and 19" (48.5cm) tall (foot to ear)

Skill Level

Experienced

Techniques

Picking up stitches on a flat piece (page 149), loop stitch (see box, page 120), mattress stitch (page 28), backward loop cast-on (page 148)

Yarn

Bulky yarn in 5 colors

Sample knit with Knit Picks Brava Bulky, 100% acrylic, 3 1/2 oz (100g), 136 yds (124m)
2 skeins (272 yds/248m) each of:
Canary (A)
Eggplant (B)
Rouge (C)
1 skein (136 yds/124m) each of:
Orange (D)
Cornflower (E)

Needles

Size 8 US (5.0mm) circular needle
Set of size 8 US (5.0mm) double-pointed needles (optional)
(See Needle Options on page 14)

Other Supplies

Stitch holder or spare needle
Stuffing
One pair of size 25mm safety eyes
Crochet hook (any size, for attaching tail)

Gauge

2" (5cm) = 7 1/2 stitches and 10 rows in stockinette stitch (knit on RS, purl on WS)

Rows 25-29: Beginning with a purl row, work 5 rows of stockinette stitch.
Row 30: K1, loop1 to last st, k1.
Rows 31-42: Repeat Rows 25-30 twice more.
Switch to A.
Rows 43-47: Beginning with a purl row, work 5 rows of stockinette stitch.
Row 48: K1, loop1 to last stitch, k1.
Rows 49-60: Repeat Rows 43-48 twice more.
Rows 61-63: Beginning with a purl row, work 3 rows of stockinette stitch.
Row 64: K1, k2tog, k to last 3 stitches, k2tog, k1 (24 sts).
Row 65: Purl.
Row 66: K1, k2tog, k to last 3 stitches, k2tog, k1 (22 sts).
Row 67: Purl.
Bind off all stitches.

Head

With A, cast on 72 stitches onto the circular needle. Place a marker and join to work in a round.
Rnds 1-5: Knit.
Rnd 6: [Loop1] to end.
Switch to B.
Rnds 7-12: Work same as Rounds 1-6.
Switch to C.

Rnds 13-18: Work same as Rounds 1-6.
Switch to E.
Rnds 19-24: Work same as Rounds 1-6.
Switch to D.
Rnds 25-28: Knit (4 rnds).
Rnd 29: [K2tog, k7] 8 times (64 sts).
Rnd 30: [Loop1] to end.
Switch to A.
Rnd 31: Knit.
Rnd 32: [K2tog, k6] 8 times (56 sts).
Rnds 33 and 34: Knit.
Rnd 35: [K2tog, k5] 8 times (48 sts).
Rnd 36: [Loop1] to end.
Switch to B.
Rnd 37: [K2tog, k4] 8 times (40 sts).

Separate Ears

Next rnd: K20, place last 20 stitches on a stitch holder or spare needle to work later.
Place the 20 working stitches onto 3 DPNs or the circular needle to work in a round.
Rnds 1-4: Knit.
Rnd 5: [Loop1] to end.
Switch to C.
Rnds 6-10: Knit (5 rnds).
Rnd 11: [Loop1] to end.
Switch to E.
Rnds 12-15: Knit (4 rnds).

Rnd 16: [K2tog, k3] 4 times (16 sts).
Rnd 17: [Loop1] to end.
Rnds 18-21: Knit (4 rnds).
Rnd 22: [K2tog] 8 times (8 sts).
Rnd 23: Knit.
Break yarn and draw tightly through the stitches with a tapestry needle.
Place the 20 held stitches onto 3 DPNs or the circular needle. Reattach the yarn to the last stitch to work in a round.
Repeat Rounds 1-23 above, then break yarn and draw tightly through the stitches with a tapestry needle.

Muzzle

With D, cast on 40 stitches onto 3 DPNs and join to work in a round.
Rnds 1-5: Knit.
Rnd 6: [Loop1] to end.
Rnd 7: Knit.
Rnd 8: [K2tog, k3] 8 times (32 sts).
Rnds 9 and 10: Knit.
Rnd 11: [K2tog, k2] 8 times (24 sts).
Rnd 12: [Loop1] to end.
Rnd 13: Knit.
Rnd 14: [K2tog, k1] 8 times (16 sts).
Rnd 15: Knit.
Rnd 16: [K2tog] 8 times (8 sts)
Break yarn and draw tightly through the stitches with a tapestry needle.

Loop Stitch

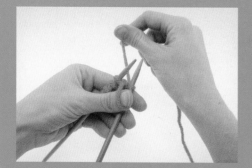

Knit 1 stitch, without slipping the stitch off the left needle. Wrap the yarn once around your thumb from left to right.

Knit through the back loop of the stitch on the left needle, and slip it off the needle.

Pass the first stitch on the right needle over the second stitch.

Feet (make 4)

With B, cast on 4 stitches onto one DPN.

Rnd 1 (work as I-cord): [Kfb] 4 times (8 sts).

Distribute stitches onto 3 needles to continue to work in a round.

Rnd 2: [Kfb] 8 times (16 sts).

Rnd 3: Knit.

Rnd 4: [Kfb, k1] 8 times (24 sts).

Rnd 5: Knit.

Rnd 6: [Kfb, k2] 8 times (32 sts).

Rnd 7: Knit.

Rnd 8: [Kfb, k3] 8 times (40 sts).

Rnds 9 and 10: Knit.

Switch to the circular needle if it's more comfortable.

Rnd 11: [Loop1] to end. Switch to C.

Rnds 12–16: Knit (5 rnds).

Rnd 17: [Loop1] to end.

Switch to E.

Rnds 18–22: Knit (5 rnds).

Rnd 23: [Loop1] to end.

Switch to A.

Rnds 24 and 25: Knit.

Bind off all stitches.

Lining

With B (or any color), cast on 6 stitches onto 3 DPNs and join to work in a round.

Rnd 1: [Kfb] 6 times (12 sts).

Rnd 2: [Kfb, k1] 6 times (18 sts).

Rnd 3: Knit.

Rnd 4: [Kfb, k2] 6 times (24 sts).

Rnd 5: Knit.

A. To attach a strand of yarn for a tail, fold the yarn in half, and pull the loop through the body with a crochet hook.

B. Pull the ends through the loop and tighten.

Rnd 6: [Kfb, k3] 6 times (30 sts).

Rnd 7: Knit.

Rnd 8: [Kfb, k4] 6 times (36 sts).

Rnd 9: Knit.

Rnd 10: [Kfb. k5] 6 times (42 sts).

Rnd 11: Knit.

Rnd 12: [Kfb, k6] 6 times (48 sts).

Rnd 13: Knit.

Rnd 14: [Kfb, k7] 6 times (54 sts).

Rnds 15–24: Knit (10 rnds).

Rnd 25: K21, BO 12 (begin binding off with the 22nd and 23rd stitches), k20 (42 sts).

Rnd 26: K21, cast on 12 stitches, k21 (54 sts).

Rnd 27-36: Knit (10 rnds).

Rnd 37: [K2tog, k7] 6 times (48 sts).

Rnd 38: Knit.

Rnd 39: [K2tog, k6] 6 times (42 sts).

Rnd 40: Knit.

Rnd 41: [K2tog, k5] 6 times (36 sts).

Rnd 42: Knit.

Rnd 43: [K2tog, k4] 6 times (30 sts).

Rnd 44: Knit.

Rnd 45: [K2tog, k3] 6 times (24 sts).

Rnd 46: Knit.

Rnd 47: [K2tog, k2] 6 times (18 sts).

Rnd 48: Knit.

Rnd 49: [K2tog, k1] 6 times (12 sts).

Rnd 50: [K2tog] 6 times (6 sts).

Break yarn and draw tightly through the stitches with a tapestry needle.

Finishing

All of the following seaming and attaching should be done using mattress stitch.

Lay the edges of the back over the bound-off stitches on the body piece, and secure in place with a few straight pins or DPNs stuck through the piece.

Beginning in one corner, seam the sides of the flap to the bound-off edge.

Turn the lining purl side out. Stuff the body piece until it's nearly full, and place the lining inside the slit in the belly, aligning the cast-on/bound-off stitches of the lining with the cast-on/ bound-off stitches of the belly. Stitch the lining in place.

Stuff the head, and stitch closed the gap between the ears. Attach the eyes, placed between the E and D stripes, and spaced 17 stitches apart.

Stuff the muzzle, and pin it to the face, between and 3 rounds below the eyes. With B, embroider nostrils onto the muzzle with 2 long, vertical stitches.

Place the head on the body, so that the cast-on edge of the head aligns with the A section of the back. Pin it in place, then stitch the head to the body.

Stuff the feet, and attach each one to a corner of the body's belly.

Weave in loose ends.

For a tail, cut two 24" (61cm) strands of each color of yarn. Fold each in half, and attach to the piñata's rump by pulling the folded loop through the body with a crochet hook (A, page 121). Pull the ends through the loop and tighten (B, page 121).

MINI PIÑATA

Body

With A, cast on 24 stitches onto 3 DPNs, leaving a tail of 8" (20.5cm), and join to work in a round.

Rnd 1: Knit.

Rnd 2: K1, kfb, k8, kfb, k2, kfb, k8, kfb, k1 (28 sts).

Switch to B.

C. After you bind off 16 stitches midway through the Mini Piñata, you will have a ring of bound-off stitches connected to 12 live stitches on one needle.

D. To make the Mini Piñata's ears, insert the I-cord through the head from side to side, so that an equal amount sticks out from each side.

Rnd 3: Knit.

Rnd 4: K1, kfb, k10, kfb, k2, kfb, k10, kfb, k1 (32 sts).

Rnds 5 and 6: Switch to C, and knit (2 rnds).

Rnds 7 and 8: Switch to D, and knit (2 rnds).

Rnds 9 and 10: Switch to A, and knit (2 rnds).

Switch to B.

Rnd 11: Knit.

Rnd 12: K1, k2tog, k to last 3 stitches, k2tog, k1 (30 sts).

Switch to C.

Rnd 13: Knit.

Rnd 14: K1, k2tog, k to last 3 stitches, k2tog, k1 (28 sts).

Distribute the stitches so that there are 8 on the first needle, 12 on the second, and 8 on the third.

Bind off the stitches on the first needle. Leave the second needle holding its stitches, and then continue to bind off the stitches on the third needle, pulling tightly between the first and third needles and binding off the last stitch on the first needle with the first stitch on the third needle.

Finish binding off the third needle, and break the yarn, leaving a tail of 6" (15cm).

With D, reattach the yarn to the last live stitch, and distribute the 12 stitches onto 3 needles to work in a round (C, opposite).

Rnd 15: Knit.

Rnd 16: K4, [kfb] 4 times, k4 (16 sts).

Rnds 17 and 18: Switch to A, and knit (2 rnds).

Switch to B.

Rnd 19: Knit.

Rnd 20: K4, [k2tog] 4 times, k4 (12 sts).

Bind off all stitches, leaving a tail of 4" (10cm).

Ears

With C, cast on 2 stitches onto one DPN.

Knit 9 rows of I-cord, then break the yarn and draw tightly through the stitches with a tapestry needle.

Finishing

Pinch the cast-on edge of the piece, and with the tail you left for seaming, stitch it together using mattress stitch.

Stuff the piece, and seam the bound-off back stitches parallel to the cast-on edge seam.

Thread the tail of the ear piece onto a tapestry needle, and insert it in one side of the head and out the other, through the last stripe of A, so that an equal amount sticks out from each side (D, opposite).

Seam together the bound-off edge of the head the same way as the cast-on edge and the back.

Weave in the loose ends, and pull several loose ends out from the piece at the rump to form a tail.

With E, embroider eyes with 2 small horizontal stitches for each, just in front of the ears.

Size
Mini piñata is 2 ½" (6.5cm) long

Skill Level
Experienced

Techniques
I-cord (page 148), mattress stitch (page 28)

Yarn
Fine-weight yarn in 4 colors, plus small amount of black

Samples knit with Knit Picks Brava Sport, 100% acrylic, 3½ oz (100g), 237 yds (217m)
Less than 1 skein (237 yds/217m) each of:
Canary (A)
Rouge (B)
Cornflower (C)
Orange (D)
Black (E)

Needles
Set of size 3 US (3.25mm) double-pointed needles

Other Supplies
Stuffing

Gauge
2" (5cm) = 13 stitches and 16 rows in stockinette stitch (knit on RS, purl on WS)

Mini piñatas are a fun bonus surprise when mixed in with candy.

Squee

In his last job, Squee was second-in-command to a fierce pirate captain. This sailor is more sweet than salty, though, so he traded in his booty for tackle and now spends his days playing catch-and-release with his fish friends.

Notes

- When binding off stitches in the middle of a row/round, always begin by working 2 stitches, then slip the first stitch over the second.
- When casting on stitches in the middle of a row/round, always use the backward loop method.
- If you will use stuffing instead of a pillow, leave out the buttonholes, and seam the top and side edges of the hat flap to the back of the body using mattress stitch.

BODY (worked bottom to top)

With A, cast on 148 stitches onto the circular needle.

Being careful not to twist the stitches, place a marker and join in a round.

Rnds 1-24: Knit.

Rnds 25-27: Switch to B, and knit (3 rnds).

Rnds 28-30: Switch to C (without breaking B), and knit (3 rnds).

Rnds 31-51: Continue to alternate 3 rounds each of B and C until you have worked a total of 5 stripes of B and 4 stripes of C.

Switch to D.

Rnds 52-71: Knit (20 rnds).

Switch to B.

Rnds 72-101: Knit (30 rnds).

Rnd 102: [K1, p1] 16 times, k84, [k1, p1] 16 times.

Rnds 103-107: Work 5 rounds same as Round 102.

Next you will bind off a section of stitches, then work the remaining stitches flat.

Rnd 108: [K1, p1] 16 times, k84, bind off to end, slipping the last stitch over the first stitch in the round (116 sts).

Rnd 109: Bind off 32 stitches (so that one stitch is on the right end of the needle and 83 stitches are on the left). Knit to end (84 sts).

Turn to begin working flat.

Row 110: K3, p to last 3 stitches, k3.

Row 111: Knit.

Row 112: Work same as Row 110.

Row 113: Knit.

Row 114: Work same as Row 110.

Row 115: K to last 7 stitches, [k2tog] twice, k3 (82 sts).

Row 116: K3, p to last 3 stitches, k3.

Rows 117-124: Repeat Rows 115 and 116 four more times (74 sts).

Rows 125-136: Work 12 rows as established, without decreases.

Row 137: K41, BO 2, k21, BO 2, k6 (70 sts).

Row 138: K3, p4, cast on 2 stitches using backward loop method, p22, cast on 2 more stitches, p to last 3 stitches, k3 (74 sts).

Row 139: Knit.

Row 140: K3, p to last 3 stitches, k3.

Row 141: K8, [k1, p1] to end.

Row 142: [K1, p1] to last 8 stitches, p8.

Row 143: K8, [k1, p1] to end.

Size
Fits a 20" (51cm) square pillow

Skill Level
Intermediate

Techniques
Backward loop cast-on (page 148), picking up stitches on a flat piece (page 149), I-cord (page 148), mattress stitch (page 28), back stitch (page 31)

Yarn
Bulky yarn in 5 colors

Sample knit with Cascade 128 Superwash, 100% wool, 3½ oz (100g), 128 yds (117m)
1 skein (128 yds/117m) of 897 Baby Denim (A)
3 skeins (384 yds/351m) of 809 Really Red (B)
1 skein (128 yds/117m) of 817 Ecru (C)
1 skein (128 yds/117m) of 1962 Brown Bear (D)
Less than one skein (128 yds/117m) of 1913 Jet (E)

Needles
Size 8 US (5.0mm) circular needle
Pair of size 8 US (5.0mm) double-pointed needles
(See Needle Options on page 14)

Other Supplies
20" (51cm) square pillow or stuffing
3 buttons (1 for eye and 2 for fastening), each approximately 1" (2.5cm) in diameter
Thread and needle for attaching buttons

Gauge
2" (5cm) = 8 stitches and 12 rows in stockinette stitch (knit on RS, purl on WS)

Row 144: Bind off as established, until 7 stitches remain on the left end of the needle. Purl to end (8 sts).

Row 145: [K2tog] 4 times (4 sts).

Row 146: Purl.

Row 147: K1, [kfb] twice, k1 (6 sts).

Row 148: Purl.

Row 149: K1, kfb, k to last 2 stitches, kfb, k1 (8 sts).

Row 150: Purl.

Rows 151–158: Repeat Rows 149 and 150 four more times (16 sts).

Rows 159–162: Work 4 rows of stockinette stitch as established.

Row 163: K1, k2tog, k to last 3 stitches, k2tog, k1 (14 sts).

Row 164: Purl.

Rows 165–172: Repeat Rows 163 and 164 four more times (6 sts).

Row 173: K1, [k2tog] twice, k1 (4 sts).

Row 174: Purl.

Row 175: [K2tog] twice (2 stitches).

Break yarn and draw tightly through the stitches with a tapestry needle.

BOTTOM HAT TIE

With B, cast on 4 stitches onto one DPN to work flat.

Rows 1–5: Beginning with a purl row, work 5 rows of stockinette stitch.

Continue to work the piece starting with Row 147 in the Body section, and work through to the end of the section.

EYE PATCH

With E, cast on 12 stitches onto one DPN to work flat.

Rows 1–7: Beginning with a purl row, work 7 rows of stockinette stitch.

Row 8: K1, k2tog, k6, k2tog, k1 (10 sts).

Row 9: Purl.

Row 10: K1, k2tog, k4, k2tog, k1 (8 sts).

Row 11: Purl.

Row 12: [K2tog] 4 times (4 sts).

Bind off all stitches.

Hold the piece with the knit side facing you and the cast-on edge to the left.

Pick up and knit 2 stitches at the top left, close to the cast-on edge.

Knit 12 rows of I-cord, then break the yarn and draw tightly through stitches with a tapestry needle.

Rotate the piece so that the cast-on edge is now on the right side, and pick up and knit 2 more stitches, on the opposite end of the cast-on edge.

Knit 32 rows of I-cord, then break the yarn and draw tightly through the stitches with a tapestry needle.

FINISHING

Lay the body piece flat, so that the beginning of the rounds faces up and is in the middle. (This is the back side of the piece.) Beginning at the bottom right corner, seam the cast-on edge together using mattress stitch.

Block the ribbed edges on the front and back of the piece by dampening

Fold the longer section of B over onto the back of the piece to determine the placement of the buttons and the bottom bandanna tie.

them and laying the piece flat and upside down to dry. (You don't need to block the entire piece—only the edges.)

Once the piece has dried, insert a 20" (51cm) square pillow, and fold the excess section of B over the top so that it overlaps onto the back of the piece. Note where the top bandanna tie (the skinny section) falls on the back. Attach the cast-on edge of the bottom hat tie to this place using mattress stitch.

Note where the 2 buttonholes fall on the back of the piece, and attach the 2 fastening buttons onto the back in those places.

Flip the pillow over so that the front faces you. Place the eye patch and

the button eye on the face. When you are happy with the placement, stitch the button in place. (Be careful not to stitch through the pillow, or else the cover won't be removable.) Next, use back stitch to attach the patch to the face (with the cast-on edge pointed up and angled a bit to the left), then stitch the I-cords in place, with the ends of the I-cords touching the top of the face section. The longer I-cord should wrap around the body and end somewhere close to one of the back buttons.

Weave in loose ends.

I tell people I lost my eye in a sword fight, but I was actually running with scissors.

King Shuffle

This self-important monarch thinks he's famous because every deck of cards comes with four pictures of him! You can tame his ego by challenging him to a game of 52-Pickup.

Notes

- When binding off stitches in the middle of a row/round, always begin by working 2 stitches, then slip the first stitch over the second.
- When casting on stitches in the middle of a row/round, always use the backward loop method.
- If you will use stuffing instead of a pillow, seam the open edges of the crown using back stitch to close the piece.

BODY

Robe

With A, cast on 148 stitches onto the smaller needle.

Being careful not to twist the stitches, place a marker and join in a round.

Rnds 1–8: Purl.

Rnds 9–11: Work according to Ermine chart (page 133), incorporating B, for 3 rounds.

Rnds 12–16: Purl (5 rnds).

Switch to C, and transfer the stitches to the larger needle as you knit the following round.

Rnd 17: Knit.

Rnds 18–50: Work according to Sweater chart (page 133) for 33 rounds, repeating Rounds 1–6 of the chart 5 times, then working Rounds 1–3 once more. (See Cables on page 152.)

Transfer the stitches to the smaller needle, and switch to A.

Rnd 51: Knit.

Rnds 52–54: Purl 3 (rnds).

Rnds 55–57: Work according to Ermine chart (page 133), incorporating B, for 3 rounds.

Rnds 58–60: Purl (3 rnds).

FACE

Switch to D.

Rnds 61–80: Knit (20 rnds).

Rnds 81–83: Work according to Hair chart (page 133), incorporating E, for 3 rounds.

CROWN

Switch to F.

Rnd 84: Knit.

Rnds 85–87: Purl (3 rnds).

Rnds 88–105: Knit (18 rnds).

Rnd 106: K23, BO 2 (begin binding off with the 24th and 25th stitches), k23, BO 2, K to end (144 sts).

Rnd 107: K23, cast on 2 stitches (using backward loop cast-on—see Notes), k24, cast on 2 stitches, k to end (148 sts).

Rnds 108–113: Knit (6 rnds).

You will next divide the crown into points, and work each separately and flat. (See Crown Configuration on page 133.) When working one point, you can either let the other stitches remain unworked on the same needle or you can place them onto stitch holders.

Size
Fits a 20" (51cm) square pillow

Skill Level
Intermediate

Techniques
Stranded color knitting (page 151), cables (page 152), backward loop cast-on (page 148), mattress stitch (page 28)

Yarn
Bulky yarn in 6 colors

Sample knit with Cascade 128 Superwash, 100% wool, 3½ oz (100g), 128 yds (117m)
1 skein (128 yds/117m) of 817 Ecru (A)
Less than 1 skein (128 yds/117m) of 815 Black (B)
2 skeins (256 yds/234m) of 804 Amethyst (C)
1 skein (128 yds/117m) of 1963 Tutu (D)
Less than one skein (128 yds/117m) of 1946 Silver (E)
2 skeins (256 yds/234m) of 821 Daffodil (F)

Needles
Size 8 US (5.0mm) circular needle
Size 9 US (5.5mm) circular needle
(See Needle Options on page 14)

Other Supplies
20" (51cm) square pillow or stuffing
Cable needle
2 black buttons, 1" (25mm) wide
5 colored buttons, 1" (25mm) wide
Thread and needle for attaching buttons
Stitch holders (optional)

Gauge
2" (5cm) = 8 stitches and 12 rows in stockinette stitch (knit on RS, purl on WS) on smaller needles
2" (5cm) = 7 stitches and 9 rows in stockinette stitch (knit on RS, purl on WS) on larger needles

Point A

Row 114a: K25, and turn.

Row 115a (wrong side): K3, p44 (remove the beginning-of-round marker), k3, turn (50 sts).

Row 116a: K3, [k2tog] twice, k to last 7 stitches, [ssk] twice, k3 (46 sts).

Row 117a: K3, p to last 3 stitches, k3.

Rows 118a–123a: Repeat Rows 116a and 117a three more times (34 sts).

Row 124a: K3, [k2tog] twice, k16, BO 2, k1, [ssk] twice, k3 (28 sts).

Row 125a: K3, p4, cast on 2, p18, k3 (30 sts).

Rows 126a–135a: Repeat Rows 116a and 117a five more times (10 sts).

Row 136a: [K2tog] 5 times (5 sts).
 Bind off on purl side.

Point B

Reattach the yarn to the next stitch in the round.

Row 114b: K24, and turn.

Row 115b: K3, p to last 3 stitches, k3.

Row 116b: K3, k2tog, k to last 5 stitches, ssk, k3 (22 sts).

Row 117b: K3, p to last 3 stitches, k3.

Rows 118b–123b: Repeat Rows 116b and 117b three more times (16 sts).

Row 124b: K3, k2tog, k2, BO 2, k1, ssk, k3 (12 sts).

Row 125b: K3, p3, cast on 2, p3, k3 (14 sts).

Rows 126b–131b: Repeat Rows 116b and 117b three more times (8 sts).

Row 132b: [K2tog] 4 times (4 sts).
 Bind off on purl side.

Point C

Reattach the yarn to the next stitch in the round.

Row 114c: Knit 50, and turn.

Row 115c: K3, p to last 3 stitches, k3.

Row 116c: K3, [k2tog] twice, k to last 7 stitches, [ssk] twice, k3 (46 sts).

Row 117c: K3, p to last 3 stitches, k3.

Rows 118c–123c: Repeat Rows 116c and 117c three more times (34 sts).

Row 124c: K3, [k2tog] twice, k2, BO 2, k to last 7 stitches, [ssk] twice, k3 (28 sts).

Row 125c: K3, p18, cast on 2, p4, k3 (30 sts).

Rows 126c–135c: Repeat Rows 116c and 117c five more times (10 sts).

Row 136c: [K2tog] 5 times (5 sts).
 Bind off on purl side.

Point D

Reattach the yarn to the next stitch in the round.

Row 114d: K24, and turn.

Row 115d: K3, p to last 3 stitches, k3.

Row 116d: K3, k2tog, k to last 5 stitches, ssk, k3 (22 sts).

Row 117d: K3, p to last 3 stitches, k3.

Rows 118d–131d: Repeat Rows 116d and 117d seven more times (8 sts).

Row 132d: [K2tog] 4 times (4 sts).
 Bind off on purl side.

FINISHING

Dampen the robe and crown areas, and lay the piece flat to dry, with the first half of the stitches in the rounds facing up, so that the crown appears symmetrical, with the buttonholes facing up.

When the piece is dry, note where the 5 buttonholes lay atop the inside back of the piece, and attach the colored buttons to these areas.

Attach the black buttons midway down the face, and spaced 16 stitches apart.

Beginning at the bottom-right corner, seam the cast-on edge together using mattress stitch.

Weave in loose ends.

I decree that you knit me!

Ermine

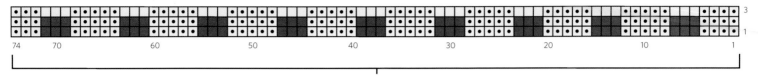

Work twice in one round

☐ Knit with A ■ Knit with B
⊡ Purl with A

Sweater

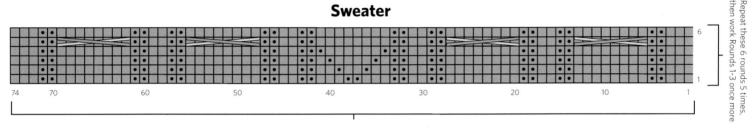

Repeat these 6 rounds 5 times, then work Rounds 1-3 once more

Work twice in one round

▦ Knit
⊡ Purl

Cable forward
(place first 4 stitches on cable needle
and hold in front, knit next 4 stitches,
then knit stitches from cable needle)

Cable backward
(place first 4 stitches on cable needle
and hold in back, knit next 4 stitches,
then knit stitches from cable needle)

Hair

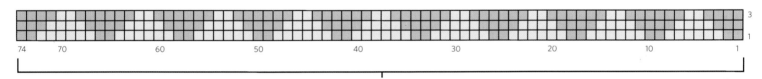

Work twice in one round

☐ Knit with D ▨ Knit with E

Crown Configuration

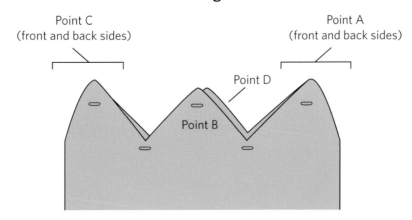

Point C
(front and back sides)

Point A
(front and back sides)

Point D

Point B

Sleepbot 3000

Her stellar button design may look high-tech, but this robot's main function is to get some shut-eye. At least her pockets are handy for carrying everything you need for your next slumber party. She promises to help you pack as soon as she wakes up.

FACE (worked bottom to top)

With A, cast on 49 stitches onto the circular needle to work flat.
Row 1: P1, [k1, p1] to end.
Rows 2 and 3: Work in established rib.
Rows 4–37: Beginning with a knit row, work 34 rows of stockinette stitch.

You will next incorporate B in the middle of the row and use the second skein of A to work the stitches at the far end of the row.

Note: When switching colors, twist the old color once around the new color on the backside of the piece before working the first stitch in the new color. (See Intarsia Color Change on page 150.)

Row 38: K12A, k25B, k12A (from second skein).
Row 39: P11A (from second skein), p27B, p11A (from first skein).
Rows 40–60: Work 21 rows of stockinette stitch in colors established in Row 39.
Row 61: P12A, p25B, p12A.
Switch to A only.
Rows 62–73: Work 12 rows of stockinette stitch.
Bind off all stitches.

BACK

With A, cast on 49 stitches onto the circular needle to work flat.
Rows 1–29: Beginning with a purl row, work 29 rows of stockinette stitch.
For Rows 30–77, work as shown in the Back chart (page 137), incorporating B, C, D, and E as shown.
Rows 78–83: Switch to A only, and work 6 rows of stockinette stitch.
Bind off all stitches.

FRONT PANEL

Before beginning this section, cut 2 yds (2m) of A, and 1 yd (1m) each of B, C, and D.

With E, cast on 49 stitches onto the circular needle.
Rows 1–9: Beginning with a purl row, work 9 rows of stockinette stitch.
For Rows 10–47, work as shown in the Front Panel chart (page 137), using separate strands of B, C, or D to work the stars, and using the strand of A to work the moon.
Switch to E only.
Row 48: Knit.
Row 49: P1, [k1, p1] to end.
Rows 50 and 51: Work in established rib.
Bind off all stitches.

Size
Fits a standard 20" by 26" (51cm x 66cm) pillow

Skill Level
Experienced

Techniques
Intarsia (page 150), mattress stitch (page 28), duplicate stitch (page 35)

Yarn
Super bulky yarn in 5 colors, plus small amount of black

Sample made with Lion Brand Hometown USA, 100% acrylic, 5 oz (142g), 81 yds (74m)
4 skeins (324 yds/296m) of 135-149 Dallas Grey (A)
1 skein (81yds/74m) of 135-107 Charlotte Blue (B)
1 skein (81yds/74m) of 135-102 Honolulu Pink (C)
1 skein (81yds/74m) of 135-158 Pittsburgh Yellow (D)
2 skeins (81yds/74m) 135-147 Minneapolis Purple (E)
Less than 5 yards (4.5m) of 135-153 Oakland Black

Needles
Size 10.5 US (6.5mm) circular needle
Set of size 10.5 US (6.5mm) double-pointed needles (for antenna)
(See Needle Options on page 14)

Other Supplies
Standard 20" by 26" (51cm x 66cm) pillow
One pair of size 25mm safety eyes
Small amount of stuffing (for antenna)

Gauge
2" (5cm) = 5 stitches and 7 rows in stockinette stitch (knit on RS, purl on WS)

Front Pocket

With C, cast on 19 stitches onto one DPN to work flat.

Rows 1–23: Beginning with a purl row, work 23 rows of stockinette stitch.

Row 24: K1, [p1, k1] to end.

Row 25: P1, [k1, p1] to end.

Bind off all stitches.

Back Pockets (make one in B and one in E)

Cast on 19 stitches onto one DPN to work flat.

Rows 1–19: Beginning with a purl row, work 19 rows of stockinette stitch.

Row 20: K1, [p1, k1] to end.

Row 21: P1, [k1, p1] to end.

Bind off all stitches.

ANTENNA

With E, cast on 8 stitches onto 3 DPNs, leaving a tail for attaching, and join to work in a round.

Rnds 1–3: Knit.

Switch to C.

Rnd 4: Knit.

Rnd 5: [Kfb] 8 times (16 sts).

Rnd 6: Knit.

Rnd 7: [Kfb, k3] 4 times (20 sts).

Rnds 8–11: Knit (4 rnds).

Rnd 12: [K2tog, k3] 4 times (16 sts).

Insert a small amount of stuffing into the piece.

Rnd 13: [K2tog] 8 times (8 sts).

Break yarn and draw tightly through the stitches with a tapestry needle.

FINISHING

Lay the back piece down purl side up, and place the face piece knit side up on top, aligning the top of the face piece with the top of the back piece.

Use mattress stitch to seam the bound-off edges of the two pieces together, then seam the two side edges of the face piece to the areas of the back side edges where they touch.

Place the front panel knit side up on top of the back piece, so that the cast-on edges align and the front panel overlaps the face piece. Seam the cast-on edges together, then seam the side edges of the front panel to the sides of the back piece. In the sections where the face piece is already attached, make your stitches just to the outside of the face piece.

Once you have finished seaming together the three main pieces, you should be able to fit a pillow inside the overlapping panels on the front.

With black yarn, embroider the eyes and mouth onto the face piece using duplicate stitch. In the sample, the eyes are each 6 horizontal stitches, placed halfway up the B section and spaced 6 stitches apart. The mouth is made with 2 horizontal stitches between and below the eyes.

Attach the front pocket to the front panel using mattress stitch, with the cast-on edge of the pocket placed 12 rows above the bottom seam of the front panel and 2 stitches to left of the stars.

Flip the robot over, and attach the two back pockets to the back panel, with the pockets' cast-on edges placed 6 rows above the bottom seam and spaced 6 stitches apart.

Attach the cast-on edge of the antenna to the top center of the robot's head, using the tail you left on the piece to seam with mattress stitch. Pull the stitches tightly when you stitch across the top seam so that the seam is even and invisible.

Weave in loose ends.

Back

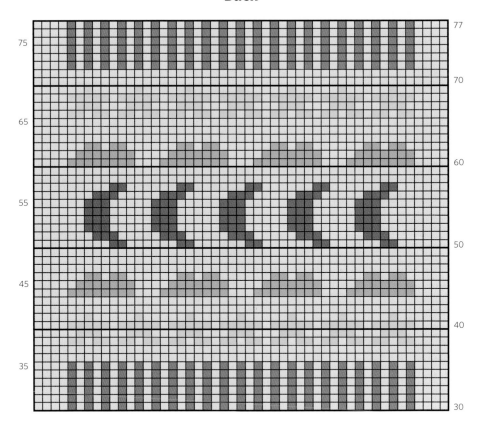

Front Panel

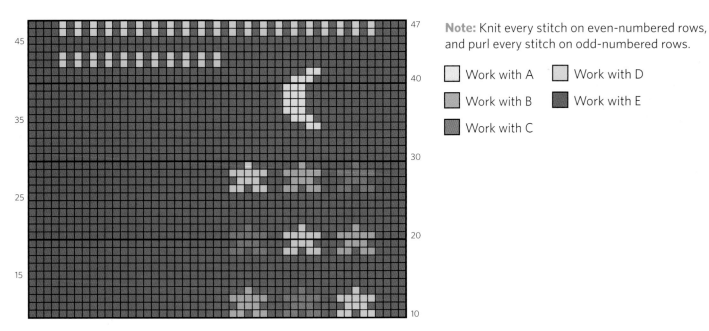

Note: Knit every stitch on even-numbered rows, and purl every stitch on odd-numbered rows.

- ☐ Work with A
- ☐ Work with B
- ☐ Work with C
- ☐ Work with D
- ☐ Work with E

Totes Adorbs

Watch out, this long-limbed creature is a real hugger! Totes wants to tag along for all your errands, and he'll even help carry stuff. Lucky for you he doesn't have bad breath.

BODY (worked bottom to top)

With B, cast on 40 stitches onto the circular needle.

Being careful not to twist the stitches, place a marker and join in a round.

Rnd 1: K20, place marker, k20.

Rnd 2: [Kfb] twice, k to 2 stitches before marker, [kfb] twice, sm, [kfb] twice, k to last 2 sts, [kfb] twice (48 sts).

Rnd 3: Knit.

Rnds 4–7: Repeat Rnds 2 and 3 twice more (64 sts)

Rnd 8: Kfb, k to 1 stitch before marker, kfb, sm, kfb, k to last stitch, kfb (68 sts).

Rnd 9: Knit.

Rnd 10: Work same as Round 8 (72 sts).

Rnds 11–13: Knit (3 rnds).

Rnd 14: Work same as Round 8 (76 sts).

Rnds 15–19: Knit (5 rnds).

Rnd 20: Work same as Round 8 (80 sts).

Switch to A.

Rnds 21–46: Knit (26 rnds).

Rnd 47: K12, begin bobble (see box), k14, begin bobble, k to end (90 sts).

Rnd 48: Knit.

Rnd 49: K12, finish bobble, k14, finish bobble, k to end (80 sts).

Rnd 50: K2tog, k to 2 stitches before marker, ssk, sm, k2tog, k to last 2 stitches, ssk (76 sts).

Rnds 51–53: Knit (3 rnds).

Rnd 54: Work same as Round 50 (72 sts).

Rnds 55–57: Knit (3 rnds).

Rnd 58: [K2tog, k7] 8 times (64 sts).

Rnds 59–62: Knit (4 rnds).

Switch to C.

Rnds 63–66: Knit (4 rnds).

Rnd 67: [Kfb, k7] 8 times (72 sts).

Rnds 68–101: Knit (34 rnds).

Rnd 102: K2tog, k to 2 stitches before marker, ssk, sm, k2tog, k to last 2 stitches, ssk (68 sts).

Rnds 103–105: Knit (3 rnds).

Rnd 106: Work same as Round 102 (64 sts).

Rnds 107–109: Knit (3 rnds).

Rnd 110: Work same as Round 102 (60 sts).

Rnd 111: Knit.

Rnd 112: Work same as Round 102 (56 sts).

Rnd 113: Knit.

Rnd 114: [K2tog] twice, k to 4 stitches before marker, [ssk] twice, sm, [k2tog] twice, k to last 4 stitches, [ssk] twice (48 sts).

Rnd 115: Knit.

3-Row Bobble Stitch

Begin bobble: In the first round, knit into the front and back of the stitch 3 times to make 6 stitches on the right needle.

In the second round, work the stitches as indicated.

Finish bobble: In the third round, work the 6 stitches, then pass the first 5 stitches over the last stitch on the right needle.

Size
Body is 11" (28cm) wide and 12" (30.5cm) long (not including arms or legs)

Skill Level
Intermediate

Techniques
3-row bobble stitch (see box, at left), three-needle bind-off (page 155), mattress stitch (page 28)

Yarn
Bulky yarn in 3 colors and small amount of accent color

Sample knit with Knit Picks Brava Bulky, 100% acrylic, 3½ oz (100g), 136 yds (124m)
2 skeins (272 yds/248m) of Cornflower (A)
1 skein (136 yds/124m) of Canary (B)
1 skein (136 yds/124m) of Rose (C)
Less than one yard (1m) of Sienna (D)

Needles
Set of size 8 US (5.0mm) double-pointed needles
Size 8 US (5.0mm) circular needle
(See Needle Options on page 14)

Other Supplies
One pair of size 20mm safety eyes
Stuffing

Gauge
2" (5cm) = 7½ stitches and 10 rows in stockinette stitch (knit on RS, purl on WS)

Rnd 116: Work same as Round 114 (40 sts).

Divide the stitches into 2 groups of 20 on either end of the needle, and bind off using the 3-needle bind-off method.

EARS (make 2)

With A, cast on 6 stitches onto 3 DPNs, leaving a tail for seaming, and join to work in a round.
Rnd 1: Knit.
Rnd 2: Kfb, k1, [kfb] twice, k1, kfb (10 sts).
Rnds 3–6: Knit (4 rnds).
Lightly stuff piece.
Rnd 7: [K2tog] 5 times (5 sts).
Break yarn and draw tightly through the stitches with a tapestry needle.

LEGS (make 2)

With B, cast on 12 stitches onto 3 DPNs, leaving a tail for seaming, and join to work in a round.
Rnds 1–8: Knit.
Switch to A.
Rnds 9–12: Knit (4 rnds).
Rnd 13: [K2tog] 6 times (6 sts).
Break yarn and draw tightly through the stitches with a tapestry needle.

POCKET

With A, cast on 21 stitches onto one DPN to work flat.
Rows 1–21: Beginning with a purl row, work 21 rows of stockinette stitch.
Row 22: K1, [p1, k1] to end.
Row 23: P1, [k1, p1] to end.
Bind off in established rib pattern.

ARMS (make 2)

Note: I recommend making the arms after assembling the rest of the pieces, so that you can adjust the length as desired.

With A, cast on 12 stitches onto 3 DPNs, leaving a tail for seaming, and join to work in a round.
Knit until desired length, stuffing as you go. (Arms on sample are 20" [51cm] long and about 106 rounds.)

Hand

Rnd 1: Kfb, k4, [kfb] twice, k4, kfb (16 sts).
Rnd 2: Knit.
Rnd 3: Kfb, k6, [kfb] twice, k6, kfb (20 sts).
Rnds 4–7: Knit (4 rnds).
Rnd 8: K2tog, k6, [k2tog] twice, k6, k2tog (16 sts).
Rnd 9: Knit.
Stuff the hand section.
Rnd 10: [K2tog] 8 times (8 sts).
Break yarn and draw tightly through the stitches with a tapestry needle.

BRACELET

With A, cast on 4 stitches onto one DPN to work flat.
Knit 32 rows, or until the piece is just a little bit longer than the circumference of an arm.
Bind off all stitches.

FINISHING

Attach eyes to the body just above the two bobbles. With D, embroider the nose between the eyes with 4 horizontal stitches spanning 2 knitted stitches.

Stuff the body about one-third full, and insert the C section into the rest of the piece to make a concave opening. Add more stuffing if necessary, so that the shape is filled out, while leaving the opening in place.

Flatten the bottom of the piece, so that the increase seams are on either side, and seam the cast-on edge together using mattress stitch.

Use the tails you left on the ears, legs, and arms to attach each to the body using mattress stitch.

Stuff the legs and attach them to either end of the cast-on seam.

Attach the ears directly below eyes, and about 12 rows up from the color change.

Attach the arms on either side of the body, aligned with the bobbles.

Flip the body onto its back, and pin the pocket in place, centered on the underside of the body. Attach the cast-on edge and sides of the pocket to the body using mattress stitch.

Seam together the cast-on and bound-off edges of the bracelet, fit it over one arm, and attach the bracelet to the arm in one place.

Weave in loose ends.

Totes Adorbs can hang on your shoulder by tucking one arm into the bracelet of the other arm. Or just tie the arms together for a shorter fit. Fashion-forward adults can wear him, too!

Knitting Essentials

BASIC STITCHES

If you're new to knitting, I recommend starting out by learning these basics on two needles. Once you are comfortable with casting on, knitting, and purling, you can switch to using double-pointed needles and a circular needle (page 13).

Casting On (CO)

The best way to start a knitting project, unless directions specify otherwise, is with a long-tail cast-on.

Based on the number of stitches to cast on, estimate how long of a tail you will need. The length will depend on the weight of the yarn and the size of the needles, but for bulky yarn and size 8 US (5.0mm) needles, I estimate about 1½" (38mm) per stitch. It's always best to overestimate how long the tail should be.

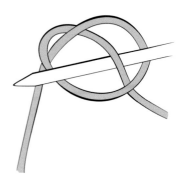

① Make a slip knot with the yarn as shown, slide the needle through the knot, and tighten. This will be the first stitch in the cast-on.

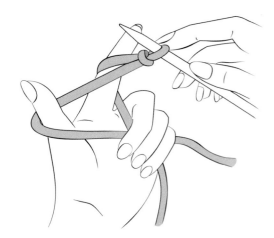

② Holding the needle in your right hand, grasp both ends of yarn in the palm of your left hand. Wrap the yarn attached to the ball around the outside of your thumb and the tail around the outside of your forefinger.

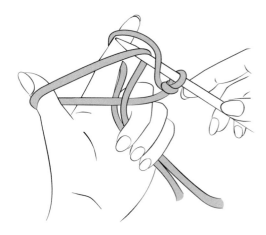

③ Insert the tip of the needle under the outer side of the yarn on your thumb from left to right.

The Knit Stitch (K)

As the name suggests, the knit stitch is the most basic stitch in knitting.

1. Hold the needle with the stitches in your left hand, and the yarn attached to the rightmost stitch. Hold the empty needle in your right hand. (For subsequent stitches, the attached yarn be will on the right needle.) Insert the tip of the right needle under the front of the first stitch from left to right, and wrap the yarn around the tip of the right needle from left to right.

2. Pull the tip of the right needle down through the stitch on the left needle, pulling the wrapped yarn out with it.

3. Slip the stitch off the left needle. You now have a new stitch on the right needle.

   Repeat Steps 1-3 as many times as indicated in the pattern, or until you have knitted all the stitches from the left needle to the right.

   When you come to the end of the needle:

   If you are knitting a flat piece with two needles, switch the right needle to your left hand and flip it around for the next row.

   If you are knitting with double-pointed needles, keep the right needle in the same position and move on to knit from the next needle that follows in the round (page 20).

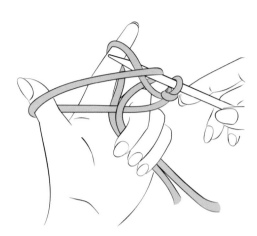

4. With the yarn from your thumb still looped over the needle, bring the tip of the needle over the inner side of the yarn on your finger, and dip it around and under from right to left.

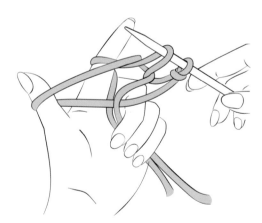

5. As you pull the needle under the yarn on your finger, bring the tip through the loop on your thumb.

   Let the yarn slip off your thumb, then insert your thumb back through the end of the yarn that's attached to the ball. As you do so, tighten the new stitch that's now on the needle.

   Repeat Steps 3-5, trying to cast on all your stitches with the same tension, until you have the required number of stitches on your needle.

The Purl Stitch (P)

The purl stitch is the reverse of the knit stitch—it happens automatically on the reverse side of knitted stitches. When knitting a flat piece, you will usually turn the piece at the end of the row and work purl stitches on the reverse side.

1 Insert the tip of the right needle under the front of the first stitch on the left needle, from right to left. Wrap the working yarn from right to left around the tip of the right needle.

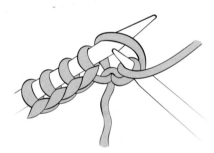

2 Pull the tip of the right needle down through the stitch on the left needle, pulling the wrapped yarn out with it before slipping the stitch off the left needle.

Repeat these two steps as many times as indicated in the pattern or until you have purled all the stitches from the left needle onto the right.

Binding Off (BO)

Most of the three-dimensional pieces in this book end with instructions to draw a loose end of yarn through the stitches to close off. (See Stuffing and Closing Up, page 25.) For flat pieces, however, the usual finishing technique is to bind off stitches.

Knit the first 2 stitches in the row as you normally would. Slip the tip of the left needle into the first of those stitches from left to right, pull it completely over the second stitch, and slip it off the needle. You have just bound off one stitch.

Knit the next stitch in the row, so that you again have 2 stitches on the right needle, and repeat until there are no more stitches on the left needle and you are left with only one stitch on the right needle.

If a pattern calls for you to bind off the purl side of a piece, you will bind off in the same way, except that you will purl all stitches instead of knitting them.

To finish off, break the yarn, slip the stitch off the needle, and slip the loose end of the yarn through the stitch. Pull tightly to secure.

Note: If a pattern calls for you to bind off a number of stitches in the middle of a row or round, start by knitting the next 2 stitches and binding them off. (Don't begin by immediately slipping a stitch off the right needle.)

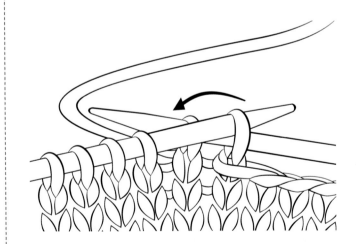

INCREASE AND DECREASE STITCHES

You need increase and decrease stitches to knit more than a rectangle or a straight tube—knitting needs curves!

Knit through Front and Back of Stitch (KFB)

Knit a stitch as you normally would, but without pulling the stitch off the left needle. Then knit into the same stitch again, this time inserting the tip of the right needle through the back half of the stitch. Once you pull the right needle and yarn through, slip the stitch off the left needle. This will increase the total number of stitches by one.

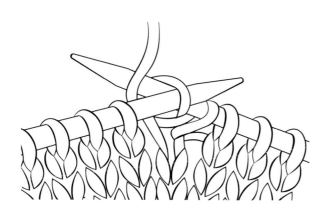

Knit 2 Together (K2TOG)

Insert the right needle under the first 2 stitches on the left needle. Wrap the yarn as you would normally do for a knit stitch, and slip both stitches off the left needle. This will decrease the total number of stitches by one.

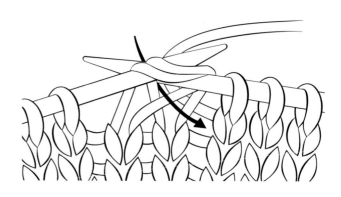

Purl 2 Together (P2TOG)

Insert the tip of the right needle purlwise through the front of the first 2 stitches on the left needle. Wrap the yarn as you normally would for a purl stitch, pull it through, and slip both stitches off the left needle. This will decrease the total number of stitches by one.

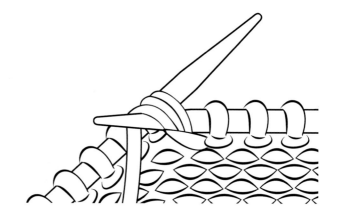

Slip, Slip, Knit Together (SSK)

Like the other decreases, Ssk will decrease the total number of stitches by one. The difference is that Ssk is a left-slanting decrease, so it's used when symmetry in decrease seams is important.

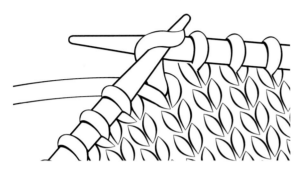

① Insert the tip of the right needle through the front of a stitch as if to knit, and slip the stitch off the left needle without knitting. Repeat for the next stitch on the left needle. You now have 2 twisted stitches on the right needle.

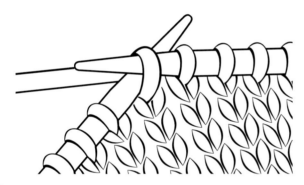

② Slip both stitches back onto the left needle so that they remain twisted.

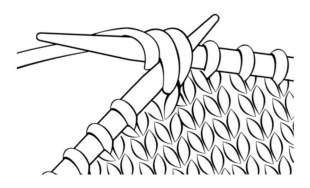

③ Insert the right needle through the backs of the 2 stitches on the left needle, and knit them together.

BEYOND THE BASICS

These additional knitting techniques will help you create the toys in this book.

Backward Loop Cast-on

This is an alternative cast-on technique that gives you a less bulky starting edge. However, in this book it's only used to add additional stitches in the middle of a row or round that has already been established.

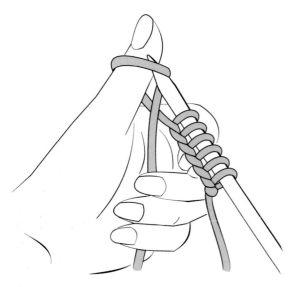

With the needle held in your right hand, grasp the working yarn in your left hand, and loop it around your thumb, from right to left. Next, insert the tip of the needle under the yarn on the outside of your thumb. Let the yarn slip off your thumb, and tighten the stitch on the needle by pulling gently on the working yarn.

Repeat this technique until you have cast on the specified number of stitches.

I-Cord

An I-cord is a skinny tube of knitting made using 2 double-pointed needles.

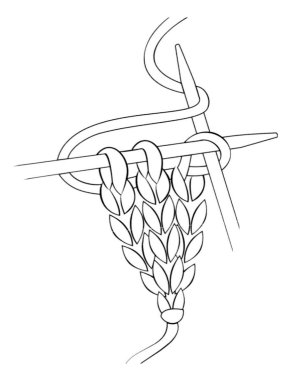

Slide the cast-on stitches to the right end of the needle, so that the stitch without the yarn attached to it is the first stitch on the left needle. Knit the first stitches using the yarn that is connected to the last stitch, pulling the yarn tightly across the back of the needle. Continue to knit to the end of the needle.

When you have knitted all the stitches from the left needle to the right, instead of turning to work the other side, again slide the stitches to the right end of the needle, and knit the first stitch using the yarn connected to the last stitch. Repeat for the specified number of rows.

Yarn Over (YO)

Yarn over is an increase stitch that makes a small hole in your knitting.

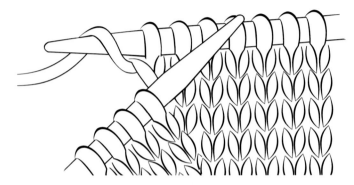

① Bring the yarn around in front of the needle in your right hand, and wrap it on the needle from front to back.

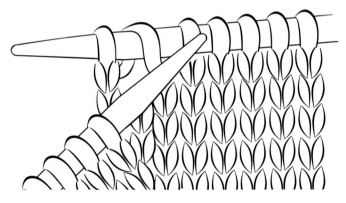

② Knit the next stitch as you normally would, while keeping the extra loop on the right needle. You'll see a small gap where you added the loop.

Picking Up Stitches on a Flat Piece

Picking up stitches along the side of a finished piece will allow you to knit in another direction and, in the case of toy knitting, it will give you a chance to add another dimension to your knitting. (Also see Picking Up Stitches on a Three-Dimensional Piece on page 32 and Picking Up Stitches around the Perimeter of a Piece on page 33.)

With the piece turned sideways, insert the tip of the needle under the first side stitch. Wrap the yarn around as you would for a knit stitch, and pull the yarn out through the stitch.

Repeat across the side of the piece, adjusting for the difference between the number of side stitches and the number of stitches to be picked up by skipping every fourth or fifth stitch.

Joining New Yarn

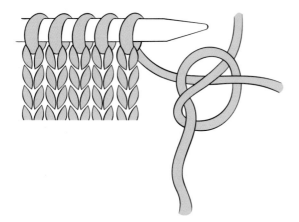

To join a new ball of yarn or a new color of yarn, tie the tail of the working yarn and the beginning of the new yarn together in a loose knot. Knit one stitch with the new yarn, then gently pull the knot tight and closer to the back, or wrong, side of the piece.

Use this technique when a pattern calls for you to switch to a new yarn color and you won't be using the first color again (or at least not again for a number of rows).

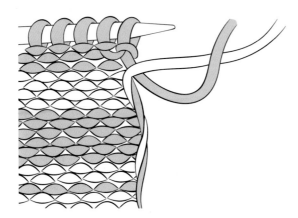

If you will use the first color again soon, as in a striped pattern of alternating colors, do not cut the first color; instead, wrap the yarns together when you start a new color, and carry the first color loosely up the side of the piece (in flat knitting) or inside the piece (in circular knitting) until you will use it again.

Intarsia Color Change

Intarsia is a technique used in flat knitting to create a color design other than a stripe, for which you need to switch colors mid-row.

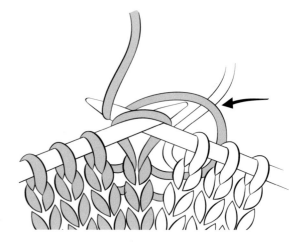

① After establishing the new color in a previous row (see Joining New Yarn, at left), the yarn for the new color will already be attached when you come to it. Before knitting the first stitch in the new color, twist the two yarns together once on the back (WS) of the piece. This will prevent a gap from forming between the two colors.

② When purling back across the same row, again wrap the yarns together before purling the first stitch in the other color.

Stranded Color Knitting

Stranded color knitting (or Fair Isle, as it's also known) is a method of carrying multiple strands of different colors of yarn along the back of a piece as you knit in the round, incorporating the different colors in your stitches as you need them. Often there will be a chart to refer to for the color pattern.

It's important to keep a consistent, relatively loose tension, without pulling any stitches too tightly, so that the finished piece doesn't pucker.

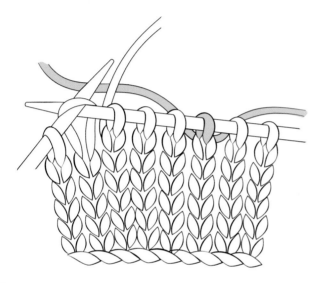

❶ As you knit, you can either hold the two strands of yarn in different hands, or you can simply drop the color that you're not working with at the moment. If there are 6 or more consecutive stitches in one color, twist the other color once around the working yarn every few stitches to help maintain even tension.

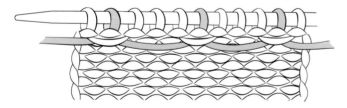

❷ After knitting a round with multiple colors, you should see the colors of yarn carried evenly across the back (WS) of the piece.

Cables

Cabling is a classic technique that allows you to make beautiful twists in your knitting. The twists go different directions, depending on whether you cable forward or backward; the following instructions demonstrate a cable forward.

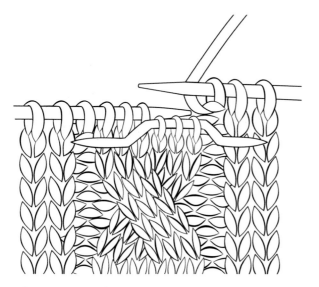

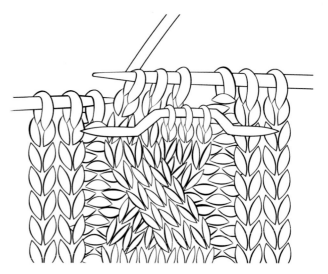

1 Slip the specified number of stitches onto a cable needle, and hold the needle in front of the piece.

2 Leaving the stitches on the cable needle unworked, knit the next set of stitches (the same number that the cable needle is holding) from the left needle onto the right.

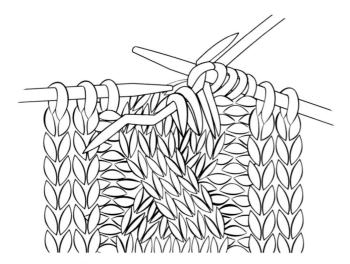

3 Next, knit the stitches from the cable needle onto the right needle, thereby twisting that set of stitches around the others that you just knit.

　　To cable backward, repeat Steps 1-3, but hold the cable needle in back of the piece instead of the front. Doing so will make the twist go in the opposite direction.

Wrap & Turn (W+T)

The technique of wrap & turn lets you turn multiple times within a single row or round, thereby lengthening one area of a piece of knitting. This results in a bend in the knitting that's perfect for making a leg that bends into a foot.

The following illustrations show a wrap & turn on the knit side; a wrap & turn on the purl side is worked the same way.

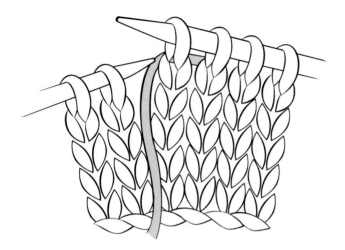

① When you come to the stitch to be wrapped, slip it purlwise from the left needle to the right, then bring the yarn forward to the front of the piece.

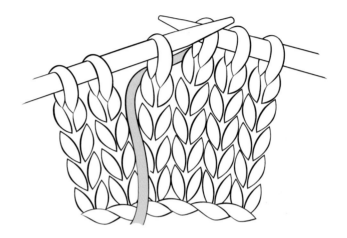

② Slip the stitch back onto the left needle. You will next turn the knitting so that the purl side faces you, and the working yarn is connected to the last stitch on the right needle. Proceed to purl the stitches from the left needle onto the right.

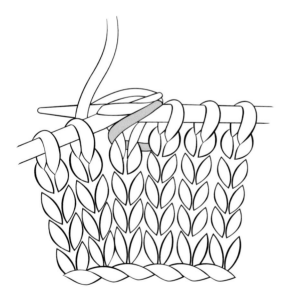

③ After working several wrap & turns in one round, you will come back around to the wrapped stitches in the following round. To make these less visible, slip the right needle through the wrapped yarn along with the stitch and knit them together.

Kitchener Stitch

The Kitchener stitch allows you to seam a live section of knitting together invisibly.

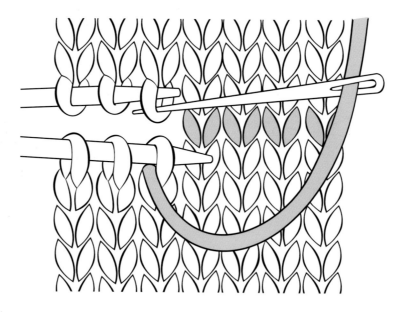

Setup

Divide the stitches equally onto 2 needles. Hold the needles parallel to each other with the working yarn attached to the rightmost stitch of the back needle.

Cut the working yarn, leaving a long tail, and thread the tail onto a tapestry needle. Insert the tapestry needle purlwise through the first stitch on the front needle, without slipping the stitch off the needle. Pull the tail through.

Next, insert the tapestry needle knitwise through the first stitch on the back needle and pull the tail through, again without slipping the stitch off the needle. These 2 stitches set you up to begin the Kitchener stitch pattern.

Seaming Steps

1. Insert the tapestry needle knitwise through the first stitch on the front needle, and slip the stitch off the needle.
2. Insert the tapestry needle purlwise through the following stitch on the front needle, without slipping the stitch off the needle.
3. Insert the tapestry needle purlwise through the first stitch on the back needle, and slip the stitch off the needle.
4. Insert the tapestry needle knitwise through the following stitch on the back needle, without slipping the stitch off the needle.

Repeat these four steps, working 2 front and 2 back stitches, until only one stitch remains on each needle.

Finishing

Insert the tapestry needle knitwise through the stitch on the front needle and slip it off, then insert the tapestry needle purlwise through the back needle and slip it off.

Weave the tail into the piece.

Three-Needle Bind-Off

The three-needle bind-off has a similar form as the Kitchener stitch, but it's simpler to do and results in a different-looking finished edge.

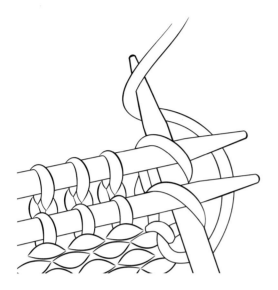

Divide the stitches equally onto 2 needles. Hold the needles parallel to each other with the working yarn attached to the rightmost stitch of the back needle.

Using a third needle, knit the first stitch on the front needle and the first stitch on the back needle together (just as in the k2tog technique, except with the stitches running front to back instead of side to side). Knit together with the following stitches on each needle in the same way.

Next, slip the first (rightmost) stitch on the right needle over the second stitch, binding off the first stitch.

Continue this pattern of knitting 2 stitches together and then binding off a stitch on the right needle, until only one stitch remains on the right needle. To finish off, break the yarn, slip the stitch off the needle, and slip the loose end through the stitch. Pull tightly to secure.

Picking Up a Dropped Stitch

Dropped stitches happen to the best of us, but they don't mean that you have to completely rip out the progress that you've made. If you notice that your stitch count is off, you may have a "run" in your knitting, where one stitch has fallen off the needle and a column of stitches has unraveled along with it.

Insert a crochet hook through the bottommost stitch that is still in place, then hook the bar that lies directly above it. Pull the bar through the stitch. Repeat for every bar above until you reach the topmost row of stitches and can place the yarn from the crochet hook onto the left needle.

How to Read Charts

Most knitting patterns use written instructions to guide you in knitting a project. In some cases, though, a chart is the best way to convey a design with more complex stitches or color patterns. Many patterns in this book incorporate charts, both for sections of flat knitting and for repeated patterns in circular knitting.

Both flat and circular charts are read from the bottom up and include row/round numbers as guides. In both types of charts, one square equals one stitch.

A chart for flat knitting represents all the stitches and rows for a given section of knitting, and may include intarsia colorwork (see Intarsia Color Change on page 150). The chart is read back and forth; right-side rows (usually knitted) are read right to left and wrong-side rows (usually purled)

are read left to right, just as you work the stitches in the pattern. The key that accompanies the chart will often tell you to interpret the same symbol one way on a right-side row and another way on a wrong-side row.

A chart for circular knitting shows a color or stitch pattern that is repeated in a round, and also sometimes repeated vertically as well. It's often used to illustrate stranded color knitting (see Stranded Color Knitting on page 151).

Because you don't turn your work in circular knitting, every round is read from right to left in a chart for circular knitting. The chart will indicate how many times you should repeat the pattern across a round and how many vertical repeats you should do as well.

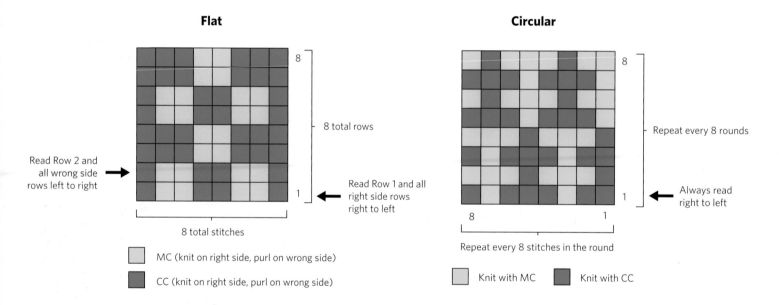

Flat

8 — 8 total rows

Read Row 2 and all wrong side rows left to right →

← 1 — Read Row 1 and all right side rows right to left

8 total stitches

☐ MC (knit on right side, purl on wrong side)

■ CC (knit on right side, purl on wrong side)

Circular

8 — Repeat every 8 rounds

← 1 — Always read right to left

8 ⎯ 1

Repeat every 8 stitches in the round

☐ Knit with MC   ■ Knit with CC

YARN WEIGHT SYSTEM

YARN WEIGHT CATEGORIES	0	1	2	3	4	5	6
TYPES OF YARN IN CATEGORY	Fingering, 10-count crochet thread	Sock, fingering, baby	Sport, baby	DK, light worsted	Worsted, afghan, aran	Chunky, craft, rug	Bulky, roving
KNIT GAUGE RANGE* (in stockinette stitch to 4")	33–40 sts	27–32 sts	23–26 sts	21–24 sts	16–20 sts	12–15 sts	6–11 sts
RECOMMENDED NEEDLE SIZES (U.S./metric sizes)	000–1 (1.5–2.25mm)	1–3 (2.25–3.25mm)	3–5 (3.25–3.75mm)	5–7 (3.75–4.5mm)	7–9 (4.5–5.5mm)	9–11 (5.5–8mm)	11 and larger (8mm and larger)

* Guidelines only: The above reflect the most commonly used gauges and needle sizes for specific yarn categories. For more information, see The Skinny on Gauge (page 17).

KNITTING ABBREVIATIONS

[ ]	Repeat actions in brackets as many times as specified	p2tog	Purl 2 stitches together
BO	Bind off	pm	Place marker
CC	Contrasting color	rnd(s)	Round(s)
CO	Cast on	RS	Right side
DPN	Double-pointed needle	sl1	Slip 1 stitch to right needle
est	Established	sm	Slip marker
k	Knit	st(s)	Stitch(es)
k2tog	Knit 2 stitches together	ssk	Slip 2 stitches to right needle and then knit them together
kfb	Knit through front and back of one stitch	W+T	Wrap & turn
MC	Main color	WS	Wrong side
p	Purl	yo	Yarn over

Resources

MATERIALS

Yarn

You can use virtually any kind of yarn to create the toys in this book. Visit your local craft or yarn shop to get inspired by the many different options available.

I chose the brands that I used to make the samples in this book for their thickness and beautiful colors, in addition to their wide availability and affordability.

Cascade Yarns
www.cascadeyarns.com

Knit Picks
www.knitpicks.com

Lion Brand
www.lionbrand.com

Spud & Chloë
www.spudandchloe.com

Stuffing & Pillow Forms

Stuffing and pillow forms can most commonly be found in larger craft stores and online.

Batt-Mart (a bulk supplier of stuffing)
www.batt-mart.com

Dick Blick Art Materials
www.dickblick.com

Hobby Lobby
www.hobbylobby.com

Jo-Ann Fabric and Craft Stores
www.joann.com

Michaels
www.michaels.com

Eyes

Plastic safety eyes may be hard to find in stores, but here are some online sellers with good selections.

Harvey's Hobby Hut
www.harveyshobbyhut.com

yeahshop (for large eyes)
www.etsy.com/shop/yeahshop

6060
www.etsy.com/shop/6060

ONLINE KNITTING HELP

Craftsy
www.craftsy.com
Virtual community and video classes on all types of crafts.

Knit Picks
www.knitpicks.com
Online retailer of yarn, needles, and other supplies, plus tutorials and other information about knitting.

Knitting Help
www.knittinghelp.com
Website with videos demonstrating basic and advanced knitting techniques.

Knitty
www.knitty.com
Online knitting magazine with lots of great patterns.

Lion Brand
www.lionbrand.com
Retailer of yarn and other knitting supplies, with many tutorials and patterns to get you started.

Mochimochi Land
www.mochimochiland.com
My website! You can find many more toy patterns to knit here, plus my blog featuring mochis knit by people like you and other fun stuff.

Ravelry
www.ravelry.com
An online knitting and crochet community, and a great resource for patterns, yarns, and technical help.

Index

A
abbreviations, 157
acrylic yarn, 12
Arthur, *84*, 85–86, *87, 151*

B
Baby Cakes, *68*, 69–71
back stitch, 31, 34
backward loop cast-on, 148
Barry & Theo, *50*, 51–55
basic stitches, 142–44
    binding off (BO), 144
    casting on (CO), 142–43
    increase and decrease stitches, 146–47
    knit stitch (K), 143
    purl stitch (P), 144
Big Mike, *76*, 77–82
binding off (BO), 144
    three-needle bind-off, 155
bobble stitch, 139
Bristles, *72*, 74–75
Buddy Boy, *102*, 103–5

C
cable needles, 16
cables, 152
Candle, 70, *71*
Capybara Caravan, *36–37*, *60*, 61–63, *64–65, 145*
casting on (CO), 142–43
    backward loop cast-on, 148
charts, how to read, 156
circular needles, 13, 14, 22
Cityzens, *92–93*, *106*, 107–10, *111, 147*
cleaning, 17
cotton yarn, 12
crochet hooks, 16

D
Dawn, *98*, 99–100, *101*
double-pointed needles (DPNs), 13, 14, 20–21
dropped stitch, picking up, 156
duplicate stitch, 35

E
embroidery, 34–35
eyes, 14, 17, 26–27

F
Fair Isle knitting, 151

G
gauge, 17

I
I-cords, 71, *71*, 148
increase and decrease stitches, 146–47
    backward loop cast-on, 148
    knit 2 together (K2TOG), 146
    knit through front and back of stitch (KFB), 146
    purl 2 together (P2TOG), 146
    slip, slip, knit together (SSK), 147
    three-needle bind-off, 155
    yarn over (YO), 149
intarsia color change, 150

J
joining new yarn, 150

K
King Shuffle, *130*, 131–33
Kitchener stitch, 154
knit 2 together (K2TOG), 146
knit stitch (K), 143
knit through front and back of stitch, 146

L
Lupe, *118*, 119–23, *124–25, 153*

M
magic loop, partial, 24
magic loop knitting, 22–23, 24
mattress stitch, 28–30
    horizontal, 29
    horizontal-to-vertical, 29
    perpendicular, 30
    vertical, 28

N
needles, 13–14
    lengths, 14
    materials, 13
    sizes, 13
Nesting Birds, *44*, 45–49

O
online knitting help, 158
Oozy & Bristles, *72*, 73–75

P
patterns, how to read, 156
picking up stitches, 32–33
    dropped stitch, 156
    on flat piece, 149
pins, straight, 16
purl 2 together (P2TOG), 146
purl stitch (P), 144

R
resources, 158
Roary, *38*, 39–43, *82*
Roland, *83*, *88*, 89–91
ruler, 16

S
Scarf, 55
scissors, 16
seams, 17, 28–31
Sleepbot 3000, *134*, 135–37
slip, slip, knit together (SSK), 147
Squee, *126*, 127–29, *129*
Squidpocalypse, *56*, 57–59, *83*
stitch counters, 16
stitch holders, 16
stitch markers, 16
stranded color (Fair Isle), 151
stuffing, 15
stuffing and closing up, 25

T
tape measure, 16
tapestry needle, 16
techniques, 20–35
    attaching eyes, 26–27
    beginning with few stitches, 21
    cables, 152
    embroidery, 34–35
    intarsia color change, 150
    joining new yarn, 150
    Kitchener stitch, 154
    magic loop knitting, 22–23
    partial magic loop, 24
    picking up a dropped stitch, 156
    picking up stitches, 32–33
    reattaching yarn to live stitches, 32
    seaming, 28–31
    stranded color (Fair Isle), 151
    stuffing and closing up, 25
    using circular needle, 22
    using double-pointed needles, 20–21
    weaving loose ends, 25
    wrap & turn (W+T), 153
Theo, *50*, 51–55
tools, 16
Totes Adorbs, *116–17*, *138*, 139–40, *141, 159*
Tree-o, *112*, 113–15

U
USS *Bubbles*, *94*, 95–97

W
weaving loose ends, 25
wool yarn, 12
wrap & turn (W+T), 153

Y
yarn, 12–13
yarn over (YO), 149
yarn weight system, 157